GREAT CHRISTIAN THINKERS

A Beginner's Guide To Over 70
Leading Theologians Through the Ages

Colin Blakely was born in Ayrshire, Scotland, and is now the editor of *The Church of England Newspaper*. After studying theology at London Bible College, he worked for BBC local radio, and was then deputy editor at *Today Magazine*. He is a writer, editor and broadcaster, and his journalistic work has taken him all over the world. He is married to Libby and they live in Epping with their daughter.

GREAT CHRISTIAN THINKERS

A Beginner's Guide To Over 70

Leading Theologians Through the Ages

COLIN BLAKELY

Hendrickson Publishers, Inc.
P.O. Box 3473
Peabody, Massachusetts 01961 - 3473

Printed in the United States of America

ISBN 1-56563-581-7

First published in Great Britain in 2000 by
Society for Promoting Christian Knowledge
       Holy Trinity Church
       Marylebone Road
       London NW1 4DU

Hendrickson Publishers' edition reprinted by arrangement with Society for Promoting Christian Knowledge.

Hendrickson Edition First Printing—January 2001

Cover design by Richmond & Williams, Nashville, Tennessee

Interior design and typesetting by BookSetters, White House, Tennessee

Edited by Shannon Goode and Dennisia Whisler

Library of Congress Cataloging-in-Publication Data

Blakely, Colin.
    Great Christian thinkers: a beginner's guide to over 70 leading Christian theologians
through the ages / Colin Blakely.
    p. cm.
    ISBN 1-56563-581-7 (pbk.)
    1. Theology, Doctrinal--Popular works. 2. Theologians. I. Title.

BT77 .B55 2001
230'.092'2--dc21   00-053997

To Libby and Aimee,
my two most favorite girls in the
whole world

CONTENTS

PREFACE

When Christ ascended after his earthly ministry, he had not left us with all the answers to the questions that were raised by his extraordinary life and message. These questions have taxed the minds of theologians for centuries but as understanding has grown so has a deeper understanding of the significance of Jesus Christ, his life, death, resurrection and ascension.

It has been said that the story contained in the Bible is so simple that everyone without exception can comprehend its message, while at the same time it is so profound that it challenges even the most brilliant minds. While many Christians are happy to live with the plain message of the Gospel story, this book is an effort to entice people to a deeper level of understanding about what our faith means and how we have come to understand it.

The style of the following pages may be light-hearted, but this should not be taken to mean that any part of the information is not intended to be serious. This is not a satire on theology, more of a simple introduction to the vast subject. Indeed, the concept first arose while we were considering the construction of a Theology Page in *The Church of England Newspaper*. We had already signed up an impressive range of theologians who would write learned articles aimed primarily at the clergy. However, some of our readers were not clergy and might not be interested in the finer points of the *Didache*, for example. So we came up with the idea of the articles you are about to read. I took a range of theologians from the early Church through to the present day and answered the questions that non-professionals might ask. It proved to be immensely popular with our readers, and so for them and for you, here is the collection.

It is my hope not only that this slim volume will explain some of those trivial worries that sometimes afflict people while listening to a sermon

('What exactly is the Nicene Creed?') but also that it will stimulate fresh thinking about theology. At the very least, it should allow you to lose that blank expression while chatting to your clergy. There is here also the opportunity to find out a little more about how the Church has developed over the last 2,000 years, so even if you are repelled by the very thought of church history, you might find this a painless way to get something of an overview.

What exactly is a theologian? Conventionally, theology is the study of the nature or being of God. Not all of the people on the following pages are theologians in the strict sense, some may be biblical scholars or important church leaders, but they have all molded the way Christians have looked on the various aspects of their beliefs. In a sense we are all theologians as we all, at some point or other, reflect on God. This book recounts how that thinking has taken place in others as well as telling how the Church has formulated its theology down through the years. The following pages reflect a personal selection of some of these leading figures and your favorite theologian may not be here. However, it is my hope that these articles will give the reader an introduction to the range of theological thought of the last two millennia.

I am indebted to a number of people, not least Andrew Carey who helped formulate the idea for these articles in the first place, to my wife and daughter for giving me the time and space to devote to writing them, to Jonathan Wynne-Jones for his comments on the manuscript and also to Liz Marsh who first had the idea of putting them all in a book. It has been a pleasure to work with her and all the staff at SPCK. Of course, while I am grateful for the input of these people, the final version is my responsibility.

There are of course hundreds, if not thousands, of other works on the subject, but there are three that stand out because they give a great overview to the whole subject. The first is Tony Lane's *Lion Concise Book of Christian Thought* and the second is the *Oxford Dictionary of the Christian Church*. I refer to many other works, often single volumes concerning a particular theologian, but have to record a debt of gratitude to these two books in particular. The third is not actually a book about the theologians, but a resource that is unrivalled: the *Christian Ethereal Library*, an Internet resource run by Wheaton College. Visit them on the web at www.ccel.org/ and you can read the full text of many of the historic works mentioned here.

It is my hope that after reading this book you will have a greater comprehension of not only what we believe as Christians, but why we believe it. Doctrine has been forged at the coalface of conflict, oppression and suffering, and many, in particular from the early Church, paid with their lives in their search for the significance of the life of Christ. We are in debt to them, and our lives and faith will be all the richer by knowing and understanding what they went through for the sake of understanding the faith.

Colin Blakely

TIMELINE

Year	Biography	Major world events
–609	Augustine of Canterbury	
614–80	Hilda	
622		Islam founded
638		Jerusalem captured by Muslims
655–750	John of Damascus	
673–735	The Venerable Bede	
739		Vikings take Lindisfarne
959		England united under Edgar
961		First monastery on Mount Athos
966		Poland converts
990		Russian Orthodox Church established
1033–1109	Anselm	
1050		Great Schism (between East and West)
1079–1142	Peter Abelard	
1090–1179	Bernard of Clairvaux	
1098–1179	Hildegard of Bingen	
1150		Crusaders launch assault on Jerusalem
1182–1226	Francis of Assisi	
1225–74	Thomas Aquinas	
1265–1308	John Duns Scotus	
1275		Marco Polo arrives in China
1330–84	John Wycliffe	
1342–1413	Julian of Norwich	
1348		Black Death in Europe
1374–1415	Jan Hus	
1378		Great Schism (between rival popes)
1431		Joan of Arc burned at the stake
1453		Turks capture Constantinople
1466–1536	Desiderius Erasmus	
1476		Caxton's presses unveiled
1483–1546	Martin Luther	
1484–1531	Ulrich Zwingli	
1489–1556	Thomas Cranmer	
1491–1551	Martin Bucer	
1491–1536	Ignatius Loyola	
1492		Columbus arrives in America
1495–1536	William Tyndale	
1497–1560	Philipp Melanchthon	
1502–55	Nicholas Ridley	
1506–52	Francis Xavier	

Year	Biography	Major world events
1509–64	John Calvin	
1513–72	John Knox	
1515–82	Teresa of Avila	
1522–71	John Jewel	
1532		Henry VIII starts Reformation in England
1542–91	John of the Cross	
1554–1600	Richard Hooker	
1555–1626	Lancelot Andrewes	
1581–1656	James Ussher	
1600		Shakespeare writes *Hamlet*
1615–91	Richard Baxter	
1620		Puritans arrive in New England
1623–62	Blaise Pascal	
1628–88	John Bunyan	
1633		Galileo condemned
1642		English Civil War
1656		St Peter's, Rome, completed
1703–58	Jonathan Edwards	
1703–91	John Wesley	
1707		Union of Scotland and England
1759–1836	Charles Simeon	
1768–1834	Friedrich Schleiermacher	
1769		James Watt patents steam invention
1776		US Declaration of Independence
1779		French revolution
1801–90	John Henry Newman	
1807		Slave trade abolished in British Empire
1813–55	Søren Kierkegaard	
1815		Napoleon defeated at Waterloo
1822–89	Albrecht Ritschl	
1840		First postage stamps
1848		Communist manifesto launched
1851–1930	Adolf von Harnack	
1859		Darwin publishes *Origin of Species*
1861		American Civil War
1865		Salvation Army founded
1870		Vatican I
1881–1955	Pierre Teilhard de Chardin	

Year	Biography	Major world events
1884–1976	Rudolf Bultmann	
1886–1968	Karl Barth	
1886–1965	Paul Tillich	
1892–1971	Reinhold Niebuhr	
1899		Boer War
1904–84	Karl Rahner	
1906–45	Dietrich Bonhoeffer	
1908–	Helmut Thielicke	
1914		First World War
1918		Church property confiscated in Russia
1926–	Jürgen Moltmann	
1928–	Gustavo Gutiérrez	
1928–	Hans Küng	
1928–	Wolfhart Pannenberg	
1929		Wall Street Crash
1929–68	Martin Luther King, Jr.	
1938–	Leonardo Boff	
1945		Second World War
1948		State of Israel established
1962–5		Vatican II
1965		Vietnam War
1967		Arab–Israeli War
1969		First man on the moon
1992		Church of England ordains women priests

PETER ABELARD

As in Abelard and Héloïse? That's the one. While he was a brilliant scholar he was also one of the most annoying characters of the medieval Church – just ask any of his contemporaries.

When did he live? He was born near Nantes in France in 1079 and died in 1142 (or 1143). Perhaps the fact that he was the son of a knight gave him a profound arrogance; perhaps it was just in his character. He made his name studying theology under two very influential figures, Roscellin and William of Champeaux, the debate at that time being on 'universals'.

You mean universalism? No, that came much later. This debate was philosophical and the two sides were split on whether these 'universals' contained any reality or whether they were just abstract concepts. For example, some said, following Plato, that there are universal realities, such as Tree, Man and Sea. So when you see a tree, for example, it derives from the bigger universal reality. But the opponents believed that 'tree', 'man' and 'sea' were only names and that the things we call by these names derived no reality from universals. The 'real' Tree had nothing to do with the yew in your garden.

Sounds complex. Indeed it was, but Abelard came up with a compromise. He said we call these things 'tree', 'man' and 'sea' because they embody characteristics of the universal. This new way of looking at things has been compared to the impact that Darwin had when he first wrote about the *Origin of Species*. For Abelard it made his reputation. In fact, it seemed to go to his head, because he quit school and set up his own classes, to which his former fellow pupils flocked. This did not go over well with his teachers, and that was a pattern that was to continue.

So he had no further need for teachers himself. Not quite. He did go to study under Anselm, but even then he could be scathing of his superiors.

He said of the great teacher: 'He had a remarkable command of words, but their meaning was worthless and devoid of all sense.' That's not a guaranteed way to impress one's elders.

How did Anselm respond? He didn't get a chance. Abelard again set up rival classes and drew away his students. However, Anselm made it clear that he had outstayed his welcome and Abelard then went to Paris.

Where did Héloïse come in? At this point. Abelard got a job as tutor to the niece of Fulbert, a canon of the famous Notre Dame Cathedral in Paris. Now Abelard was thirty-six at this point and the niece, Héloïse, was a teenager. The two fell in love and Héloïse got pregnant. This outraged Fulbert, and the pregnancy threatened Abelard's career, for he was in minor orders by this time. So he agreed to marry Héloïse secretly; but when word of her condition spread, she was sent off to a convent, much to her distress.

And Fulbert was pacified. Not a bit. He was raging. He actually went so far as to hire a gang of hit men, who paid Abelard a visit in the night and castrated him.

An extreme remedy. They don't come much more extreme than that. Anyway, Abelard took the hint and became a monk, never seeing Héloïse again, but they did correspond later in life. They were reunited in death by being buried together in Paris.

How romantic. And did Abelard finish his life quietly? No. It was after all this that he wrote his most important work: *Sic et Non* (Yes and No), and it is for this that he will be eternally remembered. Abelard introduced formal logic into the Church's theology. The idea of using logic had already been popularized by an Italian lawyer, Gratian, who built it into the canon law process. But Abelard went one step further and applied it to theology.

This was a new idea? Until that time tradition and Scripture were the two important tests in working out theology, but he said that these alone were not sufficient to answer major theological questions. Logic had to be introduced to deal with such dilemmas. *Sic et Non* followed the lawyer's method of asking questions, and this reflected Abelard's own style. He said: 'The first key to wisdom is assiduous and frequent questioning. For by doubting we come in enquiry and by enquiry we arrive at the truth.'

What was the response to this approach? At the same time there was a man called Bernard, from Clairvaux, who thought that this was the height of heresy. He tried to do intellectually to Abelard what Fulbert's thugs did to him physically. Bernard wrote to the Pope to complain and succeeded in getting Abelard's ideas condemned at the Council of Sens. Abelard was not pleased and set off to appeal to the Pope directly.

Did he succeed? He died en route. However, it is a safe bet to assume that he would not have been successful, because the Pope was a friend of Bernard, and probably listened to him. It is interesting to note, nevertheless, that one of Abelard's students, Peter Lombard, employed the same technique of using logic when he wrote his book *The Sentences*. Bernard approved of that and the book became a classic.

Don't mention Fulbert.

Most likely to say Are you getting all of this down?

Least likely to say I think Bernard might have a point here.

LANCELOT ANDREWES

He was a famous bishop? Yes, he was bishop of Winchester, but this Barking boy (who lived from 1555 to 1626), from East London, played an important part in the development of Anglicanism.

How so? Elizabeth I took a liking to him and invited him to become bishop of Salisbury and then bishop of Ely, but he turned both of these down. When James I took to the throne, he too was impressed by him and made him bishop of Chichester, then Ely and, finally, Winchester. But just before he took up the first of these posts (in 1604) he was appointed one of the translators of the Authorized Version of the Bible.

Was this just because he was friendly with the Royals? Not at all, he was fluent in no fewer than fifteen languages, so he knew a thing or two about translation. He concentrated on the first five books of the Old Testament and the history books.

But he was well connected? Yes he was. This could have been because he was educated at Merchant Taylors' and Pembroke Hall, Cambridge. But perhaps his character is best seen in the fact that he was appointed to the commission investigating Archbishop Abbot, of Canterbury.

Why was he investigating the Archbishop? Because of an unfortunate accident. The Archbishop had accidentally shot a gamekeeper while out hunting, and of course there had to be an investigation.

And he was a defender of Anglicanism. He certainly was. He first went with James I to Scotland, where they tried to get the Scots to accept the episcopacy, but it was a doomed attempt. Back home, he tried to develop a distinctive Anglican theology.

What was his agenda? He was acting against the Puritans mainly and wanted to promote what he regarded as 'a reasonable faith'. He didn't like the Puritans, so he tried to popularize the Roman heritage of the Church. He also opposed Calvin's theology, and his teaching, in particular, reflected the Roman way, especially where it concerned the Eucharist.

So he was a High-Churchman? He didn't see it like that, he saw himself as a regular Anglican, but used incense and sacrificial language at the Eucharist. What he was trying to do was to point out the middle way that identified Anglicanism.

Did he write any books? Yes, he wrote some works in defense of the king (surprise, surprise) and in support of the Oath of Allegiance, which had come in after the Gunpowder Plot. But his most famous work is probably *Ninety-Six Sermons*, which is, as the innovative title suggests, a collection of ninety-six of his sermons.

Don't mention Gamekeepers, Calvin, the Scots.

Do mention Royalty, Bible translation, the Anglican way.

ANSELM

*W*asn't he an archbishop of Canterbury? Yes, he certainly was. He held the post from 1093 to 1109, when he died. He was one of the most significant figures in the life of the Church and was famous for his work on the atonement and with his 'Ontological Argument'.

What was that all about? Anselm, unlike some of his contemporaries, used reason as a basis for belief. Most of the other scholars of the time relied only on Scripture, or the writings of the Fathers to justify their beliefs. Anselm broke the mold by using reason. And he did this most significantly in his book called the *Proslogion*, where he made the case for the ontological belief in God.

Can you explain that a bit more? Ontology is a big word that refers to the nature of being. Anselm wrote that 'God is that than which nothing greater can be conceived.' In a nutshell he argued that because we could conceive of God, he must exist, because if he did not exist he would not be the greatest conceivable being. So, he maintained that because we could think of God, it was implied in that that there must be a God.

Sounds very complex. It was, and still is. The argument he started all those years ago still excites philosophers. This Ontological Argument was in fact a development from his earlier book, the *Monologion*. In that book he tried to prove the existence of God through the existence of goodness. He said that as there were different degrees of goodness, there must be an ultimate Good, from which we calculate those different degrees.

And what was the business about the atonement? Until this time most scholars had taught that when sin entered the world the devil won rights over mankind. The death of Christ was therefore necessary to buy people back from the devil. Anselm dealt with this in his greatest book, *Cur*

Deus Homo, which means 'Why God became man'. He taught that because God is just, holy and majestic, he is offended by sin and must be offered satisfaction before he can forgive the sinner. Because Christ was sinless, God was able to accept this sacrifice and so to forgive mankind.

And how did this go down? It turned the world upside down. His argument was readily accepted and became the orthodox interpretation of the Church.

Sounds like an intellectual. Did he have a job in a university? This was just before the universities were invented. He started off life in Italy, where he was born in 1033, but after living an easy life he took off to France where he joined the monastic school at Bec in Normandy. There he met Lanfranc, who, along with others, persuaded him to take monastic vows. He was something of a protégé of Lanfranc and he eventually succeeded him as prior of Bec.

So he was a monk. He was, and after a few years as prior, where his intellectual qualities became obvious, he was made abbot.

And how did he get from there to be archbishop of Canterbury? Lanfranc had been made archbishop of Canterbury and Anselm kept in touch with him. In fact he made a few visits to England and the King, William I, was particularly impressed with him. When Lanfranc died in 1089 no one replaced him as archbishop for four years, and it was only when William II was seriously ill that he was talked into appointing a new one. He wanted Anselm, but Anselm was not particularly interested. However, cross-channel diplomacy won the day and he was consecrated in December 1093.

Did he and the king get along? Not at all. As a matter of fact Anselm spent many years in exile. He fell out with the monarch over a number of issues, especially over property disputes, the role of the monarchy in the life of the Church and in the archbishop's relations to the Pope. The King wanted to have more of a hands-on approach, but Anselm wasn't very supportive of that.

You said the king was seriously ill. Did things change when he died? It got worse. The Pope had issued a decree against the rights of lay people (such as kings) to choose and appoint bishops. He said that only the Church ought to be able to do that. Anselm told Henry I that he would not be paying homage to him, or recognizing the bishops Henry had invested. Anselm eventually tried to work out a compromise with the Pope but that backfired. He then went into exile. To make matters worse the King and the Pope then sorted out their differences, but they didn't tell Anselm!

Most likely to say It's logic . . . but not as we know it.

Not to be confused with Someone who got along with the Royals.

THOMAS AQUINAS

A *Middle Ages marvel.* He was one of the most important figures in the life of the Church, although he was not universally appreciated in his own day. Nowadays, he is regarded as a supreme teacher of Catholic doctrine.

Vital statistics? He was born in Naples around 1225, the son of an aristocratic family. When he declared that he wanted to join the Dominican order his family was bitterly opposed. So opposed in fact that his brothers kidnapped him to prevent him from signing up. They only succeeded in delaying him for a year, and he eventually made it to Cologne.

What was his contribution to theology? He studied under Albert the Great but it was when the writings of Aristotle were rediscovered that he found fame. Thomas Aquinas began to write commentaries on these ancient works and in so doing he tried to find a way to harmonize faith and reason. He followed the scholastic pattern of theologians like Abelard, Anselm and Lombard by setting up contradictory statements about an issue and finding a solution by using reason.

Was that a theological approach? It was one that had been attacked, and contemporaries of Thomas opposed his use of the technique. Scholars like Bonaventure dismissed the idea that there could be any rational knowledge of God because he is totally different from human beings. Others, like Roger Bacon and Robert Grosseteste, rejected the reason argument and turned to science for their researches. Indeed, some of Aquinas's own contemporaries regarded him as dangerous.

Did Aquinas chart his own solitary course? Not entirely. He tried to synthesize Aristotle and Augustine, and he largely succeeded. One of his greatest contributions was his 'five ways' of proving the existence of God.

11

These became famous because they asked the question of cause. Everyone accepted the 'cause and effect' phenomenon, but Aquinas went further back and asked about the First Cause.

What were these five ways? He argued that if you examine the world around you there are five features that point logically to the existence of God. These are: motion, cause and effect, the existence of things that are sustained beyond themselves, degrees of perfection, and the way that every living thing strives towards a perfect state. He claimed that all of these could cause an ordinary person to conclude that there was a creator. This was what he called 'natural theology'.

What else did he contribute? The concept of Just War was one of his main ideas, although it can also be traced back to Augustine. Aquinas taught that there were seven conditions for a Just War: the cause must be just, the just purpose must continue during combat, it must correct an injustice, it must be waged by acceptable means, it must be the last resort, victory must be assured and it must result in a just peace. These ideas are still around today and are the yardstick for determining whether a conflict qualifies as a Just War.

And has Aquinas's influence lived on to the present day? Yes, very much so. During his lifetime he faced many opponents. Some even tried to have him condemned, but these efforts came to nothing. He was canonized in 1323 and in 1567 he was declared a Doctor of the Church. The only other theologian of his stature was Duns Scotus, who found a following among the Franciscans. The Dominicans followed Aquinas, and are known as Thomists, with the Franciscans known as Scotists. As recently as 1974 Pope Paul VI declared the teaching of Aquinas as a model for theologians everywhere. To this day the Thomists dominate the thinking of the Church.

So the Church is dependent on Aquinas. Indeed. His two most important works were *Summa contra Gentiles* and *Summa Theologiae*, where he writes about the 'five ways'.

Most likely to say It's all in a Good First Cause.

Equally likely to say It's not just war if it's not a Just War.

ARIUS

Who was he then? He was an Egyptian priest who rocked the Church to its foundations. However, it has to be admitted that we know very little about him, apart from the fact that he died suddenly on the streets of Constantinople in 336.

So why did he rock the Church? Because he taught that Jesus was not the eternal Son of God, but that he was merely a heavenly being, granted the status of 'Son' as a favor by God the Father.

Ooh, heresy. It certainly was. But he was tapping into a great debate about the status of the Son. The early Church had a lot of thinking to do in the wake of Christ's resurrection, and he helped to stimulate that debate. But it was a hard-fought battle, and like an early Bob Dylan, he propagated his ideas in verse and popular song. In the red corner was Arius, but in the blue corner was his arch-enemy Athanasius, whose opposition to Arius and Arianism knew no bounds.

So what happened? The emperor, Constantine, wanted to sort out the problem, so he called a council at Nicaea in 325. Athanasius went for Arius and to prove he was right, he pulled an ace out of the deck. He used the word *homoousios* to defend the teaching that the Father and the Son were of the same substance. It worked a treat and Arius was excommunicated and banished.

What did homoousious mean? It means, literally, 'of one substance' and the dispute was whether Christ was exactly the same as God or only like him.

Was that the end of the matter? Far from it. Constantine began to have second thoughts and allowed the Arians to return. They were soon plotting and it wasn't long before they managed to have the others expelled instead. Athanasius went into the first of his many exiles, and Arius, ironically, was about to be welcomed back into the Church with open arms when he dropped dead in the street.

But his ideas did not die with him. Certainly not. Athanasius and company came back when the emperor died, but to their horror the new emperor of the East, Constantius, was an Arian, so they had to pack their bags again. A council was called at Antioch that generally went badly for the Arians, but they did not back Athanasius' use of *homoousios*. In 357 a council at Sirmium met and agreed a compromise creed, called by Hilary 'The Blasphemy of Sirmium'.

What did it say? Some people taught that the Son was like the Father in all respects. They called this the 'ousia'. They taught that the Son was *like* the Father in all ways – *homoiousios*. But Athanasius taught that the Son and the Father were the *same* – *homoousios*. There might only have been an 'i' in it, but it was an important point, because they were distinguishing between the Father and the Son.

What happened next? Later, two other councils, at Rimini and Seleucia, said that the Son was 'like the Father'. St Jerome echoed the views of many when he said, after the surprise victory of Arius: 'The whole world groaned and marvelled to find itself Arian.'

So it was a glorious success for them? They may have won the battle, but they lost the war. Many of those who were sympathetic were frightened back into orthodoxy. Orthodoxy then took hold, although Arianism resurfaced from time to time throughout the history of the Church.

Don't mention Athanasius.

Not to be confused with Aryanism (which is what Hitler was rather attached to).

ATHANASIUS

He wrote a creed, did he not? Well, there is a creed called the Athanasian Creed, but as it appears to have been written around the year 500 in the south of Gaul (France), and Bishop Athanasius died in 373, aged 83, it was probably not actually written by him.

So why is it called the Athanasian Creed? Because it is a strong defense of the orthodox doctrine of the Trinity. Athanasius, bishop of Alexandria, was an ardent defender, devoting a large part of his ministry to fighting the Arian heresy.

What was that? Arius, who was a priest, taught that only God the Father was divine, and this teaching rocked the early Church. His followers claimed that Christ was not divine, but Athanasius held that God – Father, Son and Spirit – was of one divine nature or being. He wrote books about it, the best known being De Incarnatione. He did most of his writing during his time in exile.

Exile? Why was he exiled? Because he was uncompromising in his opposition to Arianism. He was charged with conduct unbecoming of a bishop because he was so violent in his treatment of clergy who disagreed with him. But he was unpopular with almost everyone at some time or other. He was a bishop for forty-five years, but for seventeen of those he was in five different exiles.

He was unpopular with church leaders. Not just them. The emperor Constantine also had a few run-ins with him, and in one famous incident Athanasius was accused of calling a dock strike in Alexandria to cut off food supplies to his opponents.

Why was Constantine upset with him? Because the emperor wanted a united Christian empire, and he worked out a way to reconcile repentant

Arians with the Church, and so extend his power. Athanasius wouldn't participate: he was having none of it.

So what does this creed actually say? It paved the way for the Nicene Creed, and was important because it made clear the doctrines of the Trinity and the incarnation. It was very wordy and it was for this reason that it was not used very much.

What else was he famous for? He used to write Easter letters to the Egyptian churches. One of these, the one he wrote in the year 367, is the first time the list of books agreed to be the genuinely holy ones in the New Testament was identified. This 'Canon' (as it is technically known) is the one we use today, so he was very influential in that.

Anything else? Yes. Up until then everyone had been thinking and arguing about the divinity of Christ, and Athanasius certainly had a lot to say on that subject, but he also had a wider horizon. No doubt his sojourn in the desert gave him time to think. And one of the things he thought about was the Holy Spirit. People had so far taken the role of the Holy Spirit for granted. He broke new ground by writing on this aspect of theology.

Why did he go to the desert? It was one of his exiles, and while there he met the monks who lived there. He wrote a life of St Antony and this book led to the spread of the idea of monasticism in the West.

So he was an important fellow. Yes, of course. It has been said of him that if it hadn't been for his stubbornness in opposing Arianism, the heretical movement would have been far more successful.

Don't mention Arius, dissident clergy, anyone else who gets on his nerves.

Do mention One being, St Antony, the Canon, monks.

AUGUSTINE OF CANTERBURY

The first archbishop of Canterbury? Yes, he was. He was sent here by Pope Gregory the Great and landed in Kent in 597. While en route he wrote to Gregory indicating his desire to turn back, but Gregory encouraged him and he continued his journey.

It was Gregory's desire to convert England? Yes, the famous story of Bede goes that Gregory saw some young fair-haired lads in Rome and asked who they were. When told of the origin of the Saxon slaves, he replied: 'Non Angli, sed angeli' ('Not Angles, but angels'). This alerted him to the existence of the Angles, and so he summoned Augustine for a new mission.

What were Augustine's qualifications for this job? We don't know much of his early life, but he comes into the frame when he was prior of a Benedictine monastery in Rome, and it was probably this that singled him out for the mission. Pope Gregory had himself created this monastery of St Andrew in Rome, so he would have known Augustine well.

Was Augustine a great missionary figure? Look at the Church in England today for evidence of that. The historians are, however, cautious about him: it seems that it was Gregory who was the towering figure, and Augustine apparently wrote to him for advice on the most trivial of matters; but all that pales into insignificance when we look at his achievements.

And what were they? He arrived in England to re-establish the Church here. Fortunately for him Ethelbert's wife was a Christian, and they gave him a residence in Canterbury where he set up a monastery with the 40 monks who travelled with him from Rome.

Who was Ethelbert? He was the king of Kent, and when he converted to Christianity, suddenly Augustine was a figure of great importance and many also converted to Christianity. It is said that on one day alone Augustine baptized over 1,000 people in the River Swale.

He was successful at that then. Yes he was, but on other matters he was less than successful. When he arrived here there already was a church in existence – the Celtic church – and he tried to bring them into line with Roman practice and belief. To this end he held a conference at Aust on the Severn in the year 603, but he failed miserably. Nevertheless, he carried on with his mission to the Angles.

What did he do next? He sent one of his monks, Justus, to preach on the other side of the Medway and he gave him the title of Bishop of Rochester. That was in 604, the same year as he sent Mellitus to evangelize the East Saxons. He got the title of Bishop of London.

Was that the end of the story? Almost, for Augustine. He died either in the same year or at the latest by 609 (the records from this period are vague, as you might imagine), but anyway not before he consecrated Laurence as his successor at Canterbury.

Not to be confused with Augustine of Hippo.

Most likely to say Put that in the 'too hard' tray. You cannot be serious.

AUGUSTINE OF HIPPO

Of *Hippo?* Not the animal. Hippo was a town on the coast of Algeria.

How come he ended up in Britain, then? Not Augustine of Canterbury, this Augustine was a much more influential theologian than the English missionary.

Isn't this the one everyone criticizes for being anti-sex? True he had a very developed sense of sin, especially his own. In his youth he was a great sinner! In his book, *Confessions*, he says that the fact that he was tempted to sexual sin was not a conundrum to him. In fact, it was entirely understandable. What was a profound problem was his encounter with the pear tree.

The pear tree? Yes. When he was a boy he stole some fruit, although he had no earthly need for it. It was this perversion of his character that he found difficult to understand. As far as sexual sin was concerned, that was obvious, but here there was no apparent reason for his behavior.

But he was tempted in that way? He took a mistress at the age of seventeen, who bore him a son; later he abandoned her and was betrothed to a twelve year-old heiress found by his mother. He took a further mistress before the religious crisis which finally led to his baptism by another famous Church father – Ambrose.

I see what you mean. Augustine (who lived from 354 to 430) was one of the most fascinating characters in Christian history. The much imitated but never matched *Confessions* forms one of the earliest autobiographies. He did more than anyone since the New Testament was written to set out Christian doctrine in opposition to the heresies of the early Church, including Donatism and Pelagianism. He developed a whole political philosophy, preceded Descartes with the formula 'I think therefore I am' and came up with a very interesting theory of time . . .

He was a busy man. In addition to this he found time to address the Trinity, advance a highly influential doctrine of original sin . . .

Did he get any sleep? You can see how important he is.

Yes, but put it all in a nutshell. At the heart of his influence lies the fact that he so powerfully advanced St Paul's teachings. The emphasis on original sin and the helplessness of man without God's grace prompting faith became the theme of the reformers 1,000 years later. And there's more . . .

You said he wrote the original Confessions – *did he write anything else?* His book *City of God* was an instant best-seller and has gone down in history. There was a great feeling of shock when Alaric, king of the Visigoths, ransacked Rome. People said it was because the Romans had abandoned the old gods. But Augustine said that there were two 'cities': the City of God, made up of people who believed in him, and the City of Man (meaning people in general), made up of pagans. The former had nothing to lose by the destruction of the temporal city, for their hope was elsewhere. This was not their home, in other words.

So he sorted out the Christians from the pagans. He actually went further than that because he talked about 'two Churches'. He taught that joining the Church, and even being baptized, were not enough to make a person a Christian. So he started the idea of the 'invisible' Church (of true believers) against the 'visible' Church. He wrote: 'Many whom God has the Church does not have, and many whom the Church has God does not have.'

Tell me more about Augustine's sin, the theology is too complicated. At one point he said: 'Give me chastity, but not yet.' But while he fully appreciated his own sin, and his inability to do anything about it, this brought him into conflict with a British abbot, Pelagius. The latter taught that man's good deeds were required by God, but for Augustine salvation was a free gift, not something to be earned.

Sounds like a very holy man . . . He was, but he probably would not have admitted it. He was also the first person to introduce the idea of a group of celibate monks living together serving a church. All of these things were to have a profound influence on the rest of the Church, not just in North Africa.

What sort of things did he influence? Well, if you remember Calvin's idea for running Geneva – he wanted to run it as a theocracy – that idea came from Augustine. Luther was also heavily influenced by him.

And you say he is influential even today? Very much so, but he is as much a victim of political correctness as St Paul in certain circles. Some modern theologians just don't accept his emphasis on original sin and try to emphasize 'original blessing' instead.

What's wrong with that? Just look around at the world and then take a look at yourself. Isn't that enough evidence for Augustine's very real sense of sin and the sinfulness of the whole human race?

Fair enough. But with the questioning of any real sense of sin, his critics also question the entire redemption tradition that he did so much to emphasize.

Best remembered for Confessions and City of God.

Best quotes To err is human, to persist in error is devilish. You have made us for yourself and our heart is restless till it finds its rest in you.

Not to be confused with Augustine of Canterbury.

Don't mention Pelagius.

Do mention Two kingdoms. Two churches.

KARL BARTH

He was a leading modern theologian? Yes. He was Swiss and lived from 1886 to 1968; his has been described as the most significant theological work since the Reformation.

What was that? His massive, but unfinished, work called *Church Dogmatics*. This was a huge task, creating a modern systematic theology, and is still invaluable, even though ill health prevented him from finishing the last volume, *The Doctrine of Redemption*.

What was his theology? He has been called a neo-orthodox, because he broke with liberalism, which was the prevailing mood of the Church. After the First World War Barth was no longer a so optimistic as his contemporaries. So his theology moved in a new direction, although it was really an old direction. He now advocated a more emotional and spiritual approach to theology.

In what way? He drew a distinction between religion and revelation. His idea was that the only way to really know God was to receive, by the grace of God, a revelation from God. Our efforts at discovering God would be fruitless, because it was only by God's revealing of himself that we could know anything. And the only revelation that meant anything in human history was the revelation of Jesus Christ.

Was that a popular stance? Not universally. What this meant was that there could be no meeting of the minds with other religions, if they were chasing in the dark while Christians were basking in the light. His fellow theologians also questioned this: some thought he was too soft and others thought he was too hard. Schleiermacher, for example, thought that religion had to be verifiable in the lab, and so he disagreed with Barth's inner journey.

So where did Barth's ideas come from? He was influenced by Luther and Calvin but also by Kierkegaard, the Danish existentialist. It was when he published his commentary on the Book of Romans that he was catapulted to fame worldwide.

What did that say? He reaffirmed the old teachings, including the sovereignty of God, original sin, revelation. His writings were radical, mainly because he refused to agree that Christianity was a religion comparable to other religions.

What was his background? He came from a Swiss Protestant family and served as a pastor in Switzerland for twelve years. He then moved to Germany where he began his monumental work on *Church Dogmatics*.

What exactly is systematic theology? This is a discipline of examining all the various strands of Christian theology and applying the findings to every aspect of life and the various branches of theology. Barth started writing his work in 1932 and it continued until his death. It was only interrupted by the Second World War.

What was his situation there? He spoke out against Hitler. It was because of his Swiss citizenship that he escaped serious censure, at least at first. But this also affected how he saw theology. He rose up against liberalism and the persecution of the Jews. He also reacted against natural theology, arguing that people must simply accept the fact that they are sinners and repent of it. No debate. The Nazis kicked him out of his university and he was forced to move to Basel in Switzerland where he became professor of theology.

But he was still involved in the German scene? Yes he was, he was the man mainly responsible for the Barmen Declaration, in which the German churches apologized for not standing up to Hitler. Barth was deeply concerned about this because at first, although he joined up with the Confessing Church, which did oppose Hitler, he felt that the Church should not get involved with politics. Later, he changed his mind and said it was important to speak out.

Famous quote He gave the summary of his theology as follows: 'Jesus loves me, this I know, for the Bible tells me so.'

Not to be confused with Lionel Bart (who wrote *Oliver*, which was no justification for anything).

RICHARD BAXTER

*O*ccupation? He was chaplain to Cromwell's army during the English Civil War and is famous as a Puritan writer and theologian. However, he did not fully agree with Oliver Cromwell's theology and this set the two apart.

When did he live? 1615–91. He was born in Rowton, Shropshire, and had a sporadic education. At an early point, having gained the opportunity to study in London thanks to Sir Henry Herbert, he displayed his Puritan credentials. He was a tender soul with his opinions and he was so sickened at what he regarded as the frivolity displayed by his fellow students that he decided he would do much better by going home and studying theology on his own. However, he was clearly bright enough for the bishop of Worcester to ordain him in 1638. The question is, did the bishop know of his enthusiasm for dissent?

And did he? We shall never know, and it is possible that at this stage Baxter was still developing his theology. He had met with two other theologians, Joseph Symonds and Walter Craddock, who encouraged his disillusionment with the episcopal pattern of the Church of England. But it was after he was appointed assistant minister at Bridgnorth that he became more aware of Nonconformity.

And the bishop didn't object? He didn't seem to, but then Baxter didn't cause a fuss at this time, he just quietly got on with his work and impressed everyone by working closely with the ministers of other churches in the area, in an early effort at a local ecumenical project.

When did he come into contact with Cromwell? He moved in 1641 from Bridgnorth to Kidderminster, where he was the curate, and after the Battle of Naseby in 1645 he became chaplain to Whalley's regiment. It was at this point that the differences began to emerge. Baxter didn't like the republican movement and tried to undermine it from within, but when that didn't work he resigned and went off to write his most famous book, *The Saints' Everlasting Rest*.

And did that take him back into the bosom of the Church? Not at all. You see, he may have been against the republicans, but he was still unhappy with episcopal practice. So when Charles II was restored to the throne (something Baxter had campaigned for) he was offered the bishopric of Hereford. To the shock and surprise of many he turned it down on a matter of principle. This did not go over well with his superiors and they promptly banned him from any job in the Church.

And that was the end of the story. Not quite. He was also involved in the Savoy Conference. This was held in the Savoy in the Strand in London. The purpose was to review the Book of Common Prayer and Baxter was given a part to play there. What he wanted to achieve was to allow as many of the Nonconformists as possible to stay in the Church of England, but he missed out on that one. His fellow Anglicans were, not surprisingly, indignant about someone who had the audacity to turn down the job of bishop. He also proposed an alternative service book that was rejected, and his bid to ensure that clergy who were ordained in dissenting churches would not have to be 're-ordained' by the Church of England likewise fell at the conference.

A bad day for the Puritans. It certainly was. In all 2,000 clergy were forced to leave the Church after the Conference, but for Baxter, who then devoted his time to writing, things took a turn for the worse.

What happened? He wrote a Paraphrase of the New Testament, and his enemies, incensed by this, had him hauled before the notorious Judge Jeffreys, who called him a dog. His critics claimed that Baxter was libeling the Church of England in this work and the judge agreed. He said that it would be no more than justice to whip such a villain, although he only fined him 500 marks. However, Baxter couldn't produce the money immediately, so he languished in jail for 18 months until the fine was paid.

Least likely to say Play by the rules.

Don't mention Judge Jeffreys. On any account.

THE VENERABLE BEDE

He was a great historian, wasn't he? Yes, but he was much more besides. In addition to being England's first historian, he was also a theologian, a computist and a hagiographer.

Computist? He was very astute with numbers and mathematics. It was he who first popularized the calendar that took as its baseline the birth of Christ. And it was also he who first worked out the formula for calculating the date of Easter. In fact, he was so enthusiastic about this part of his life that he added his own chronology of the history of the world at the end of his mathematical works.

And what is a hagiographer exactly? That is someone who writes up the life of a saint, a sort of blessed biographer. He wrote up the life of St Cuthbert not once but twice (once in verse), and this work helped popularize St Cuthbert throughout Europe.

He was a theologian as well? Yes, he was quite clever. He was one of the first people to translate the Bible into English and he also wrote commentaries on some of the books of the Bible. These attempted to extract the spiritual truth of the Bible by using an allegorical method of reading the Bible, a style that remained popular for several hundred years. It was the style popularized by the Antiochian school. So, all in all, he was much more than a historian, although that is what he is best known for nowadays.

What was the name of his famous book? You're probably thinking of the *Ecclesiastical History of the English People*, which he completed in AD 731 – four years before his death at the age of sixty-two. This book was ground-breaking in that he was concerned with facts, unlike some of his contemporaries who liked a good story. That is the book most people associate him with. While he did write much more, not much else survives.

And he is forever connected with the north of England? His bones were buried in Durham, but he started as an oblate at Wearmouth monastery when he was just seven. When the monastery at Jarrow was founded in 682 he transferred there and remained there until his death, with only brief visits elsewhere.

What were the main themes of his ministry? He seemed to put a great deal of stress on 'episcopal visitation' (the need for the bishop to visit the flock). He also focused on the importance of confirmation and he encouraged frequent celebration of the Eucharist in church life. In this he thought he had found the answer to the evils of society.

So when did he become 'Venerable'? That title was given to him about a century after he died, and in 1899 Pope Leo XIII declared him a 'Doctor of the Church'.

Least likely to say I heard this one from a friend.

Most likely to say Are you getting all this down.

Not to be confused with Worry Beads.

BERNARD OF CLAIRVAUX

He was a quiet and gentle monk, with a poetic streak, was he not? Shy and retiring are not words that one could associate with Bernard. He was a towering figure and an immensely important one in the world of the twelfth century.

Not quiet? On the contrary, he was extremely vocal and even provoked the Second Crusade. He was born to a noble family near Dijon in 1090 and later he joined the Cistercian monastery at Citeaux. He proved to be rather important early on and he was asked by the abbot three years later to find a venue for another monastery. He settled on Clairvaux (hence his name) and he built it into one of the main centers of the Cistercian order.

Was he a popular abbot? He was and he was also a convincing speaker. It was said that when he went out trying to find new candidates for his monastery mothers used to hide their sons because he was so persuasive. Indeed, it was largely due to him that people were convinced of the merits of waging the Second Crusade, and when it all ended in disaster he emerged relatively unscathed, laying the blame on the Crusaders' lack of faith.

And people believed him? Not at first; there was complete disbelief at the failure of the Crusade. When the Christians were ambushed in Damascus people looked for a reason. Bernard gave them a scapegoat: he said that the Greeks were now a problem. That was why the Fourth Crusade set off to take over Constantinople in 1204. That was successful but it was also the last straw for the Orthodox, and they cut the last of their links with Rome. Despite the setback of the Second Crusade, Bernard continued to impress his followers. Perhaps not surprising from a man who once said: 'All things are possible to one who believes.'

He had a charming way with words. He certainly did, and this earned him the nickname 'mellifluous', which actually means sweet as honey. But he also had an edge to his character. Just ask Abelard.

What happened there? Peter Abelard was just one of many to get the sharp end of his tongue. Bernard called him a 'son of perdition' for apparently undermining the atonement. In fact, Bernard was so cross with Abelard's style of doing theology and his use of reason that he had him condemned at the Council of Sens in 1140.

So his fellow church leaders paid attention to him. They certainly did. And, not least, the Pope paid attention to him. But there was a story there.

What was the story? There was a rivalry between two popes, Innocent II and Anacletus. Bernard backed Innocent, and when he won the battle, Bernard's order of monks suddenly found that they were enjoying a wide range of new privileges from the new Pope. He knew who his benefactor was.

He sounds like he was a busy man. Did he spend much time at his monastery? He certainly did. He also wrote and preached a great deal. He wrote no fewer than eighty-six sermons on the Song of Solomon and he wrote a number of important works on monasticism. In fact, he was so important that he is regarded as the 'last of the Fathers'. He was essentially a spiritual writer but he wrote many serious academic works, including one on the question of good works and sin, called *Grace and Freewill*.

Did he live a typical monastic lifestyle? Yes he did. The Cistercians lived a hard life, and he eventually died (in 1153) from his strenuous self-denial.

Famous quote The mortified man is able to suck honey from the rock and oil from the flinty stones.

Most likely to say Listen to your father.

LEONARDO BOFF

He was involved in the Liberation Theology movement, was he not? Yes. One of his most famous books earned him a censure and a ban on his preaching from the Vatican, but he was nevertheless profoundly influential in the field of Liberation Theology.

What did he have to say? Boff was perhaps a product of his environment: being a Brazilian Franciscan theologian (born in 1938) he was sensitive to the needs of the poor. The teaching of the Liberation Theology movement that was widespread in Latin America from the 1960s was taken up by him with a great sense of eagerness. But the Church was not so convinced by the movement, or by Boff's ideas.

Which were? He believed that when Christ was revealed it was not words so much as *the Word*, the liberation of God's people, that was announced. Therefore, it follows that the Church should be more concerned with radical action than with the content of sermons. But what caused greatest controversy was his view that the Church had fossilized over the years and was now in need of great reform itself.

And he was the man to do that? What he was arguing for was a radical reform, much greater than could be achieved by one man. This was despite his own impressive credentials. He was ordained in Brazil but studied in Würzburg, Louvain, Oxford and Munich, before becoming professor of systematic theology in Rio. Boff talked about the 'Iglesia popular', the 'people's Church'. He believed that the Holy Spirit would empower the Church much more than any clerical hierarchy ever could. And so he wanted to limit the role of the hierarchy.

But did he not expect a cool reception to that idea? Perhaps, but when theologians are arguing over points of theology like this they are arguing for

31

what they see as the truth, and in this case Boff believed that the Church had simply forgotten the truth with the passage of time. Over the centuries the Church had become too clerical in its approach and was now as oppressive as the powers that he believed Christ had come to deliver us from. So what the church authorities had to say was all very well, but he was making a wake-up call to the Church. If they didn't hear him, that would be their fault, not his.

And what was the reaction? Some would say it was predictable. He was called to the Vatican, who were worried at what they saw as the 'Liberation Theologians supping with Marx, only with a long spoon'. This was not something that Pope John Paul II was going to put up with – after all, he had first-hand experience of living under Communism in his native Poland. The powers-that-be wanted this movement to be more circumspect and to tone down its advocation of violence. While it did the latter the International Theological Commission issued a ruling on Liberation Theology and summoned Boff to the Vatican for an interview. It was clearly not an issue that could be settled over a glass of port at their club, for Boff was then banned from speaking and publishing, although his ban only lasted a year.

They were dogmatic about the subject, then. The Church clearly had problems with Liberation Theology, although at first sight some of these might seem more to do with how they should handle it from a PR perspective rather than with theological issues. The Second Instruction from the International Theological Commission, for example, toned down the outright opposition, but it nevertheless scarcely mentioned Liberation Theology by name.

So things got better for the Liberation Theologians? Not quite. Another leading figure in the movement, Gustavo Gutiérrez, was himself banned from preaching in 1994, so the issue has not yet died down.

What else did Boff write? His most influential books include *Jesus Christ Liberator* (1972), *Church: Charism and Power* (1981), *St Francis: A Model for Human Liberation* (1985) and *The Maternal Face of God* (1988).

Most likely to say Don't mention the Church and power in the same breath.

Least likely to say We have a lot to learn from the Church in the West.

Dietrich Bonhoeffer

The sad story of the German pastor. And it was more than sad, tragic even. But he was also a controversial theologian. Shall we start with the Nazi angle?

What happened? Bonhoeffer was born in 1906, his father a professor of psychiatry in Breslau, which was then in Germany but is now in Poland. His father and all his brothers were agnostics and he went against the pattern in choosing to study theology. After his training at Tübingen and Berlin, he went on to become a Lutheran pastor. However, when Adolf Hitler began to rise to power, Bonhoeffer spoke out against him and his National Socialist Party.

He didn't approve of them? No he didn't, and he spoke out quite literally. In 1933 he went on radio and denounced the Nazis, but he found he was cut off before he finished his talk. That was an omen of what was to follow.

Was he arrested? No. But only because he left the country. He went to England to pastor a German congregation there. Back in Germany his fellow colleagues who opposed the Nazis set up what they called the 'Confessing Church'. Not surprisingly, the Nazis hated them. When Bonhoeffer returned to Germany in 1935 he found himself restricted in what he could do. At first they stopped him lecturing, but then he was forbidden to preach, write or publish.

How did he respond to that? He joined the resistance and even helped in a plot to assassinate Hitler. He was on a lecture tour of the USA when war broke out, and so he returned to Germany. He was friendly with the English bishop of Chichester, George Bell, and tried to mediate between his fellow Germans, who were opposed to Hitler, and the British government.

Was he successful? No. He was arrested in 1943 and taken into custody. The following year when the Gestapo raided his home they found the evidence they were looking for. On April 8, 1945 (just months before the end of the war) he was hanged, and his famous last words were: 'This is the end – for me the beginning of life.'

Now, what did you say about his theology being controversial? He advocated a 'mature' faith in the modern world. In particular, he wanted a 'religionless' Christianity. Some took this to mean that he, like Bultmann, wanted to get rid of the miraculous aspect of the faith, but he said he wanted to communicate his faith to a world that was not religious.

He wasn't against the miraculous? Not entirely, but he was opposed to those who said that Christianity was just a crutch for bad times, or that it was an easy answer to all the unexplained problems of life. He upset some evangelists, who he thought tried to convert people by making them aware of their sin. Bonhoeffer thought that this was 'an attempt to put a grown-up man back into adolescence'.

And he was influential even after his death? He certainly was. One of his most famous books, *Letters and Papers from Prison*, was published posthumously and later caught the imagination of scholars. For example, when Bishop John A. T. Robinson wrote his book *Honest to God*, it was seen as drawing on both Bonhoeffer and Bultmann, although Bonhoeffer also disagreed with Bultmann.

What did they disagree on? He thought Bultmann made two errors. First, he went too far and, second, he didn't go far enough.

Stop being clever. First, then, he thought Bultmann wanted to strip away everything from Christianity leaving only the essence. That was going too far. But second, Bonhoeffer claimed that Bultmann was not going far enough. The problem wasn't myth, he said, it was religion itself. People might have problems accepting the miraculous parts of Christianity, but they had as many problems even accepting the existence of God. So his answer was a 'religionless' Christianity.

What on earth did that mean? He didn't like the idea that 'this world is not my home'. He said that the world was important and we neglect it at our peril. He also reacted against the individualism of the modern Church, which stressed that salvation was personal. And he wanted Christians to have a wider worldview, and not just to be concerned with 'spiritual' things.

Least likely to say The government can do no wrong.

Most likely to say Be grown-up about your faith.

MARTIN BUCER

Was he another reformer? Not just another reformer, he is known as the 'father of Calvinism'. Although he was born in Alsace, he later settled in Strasbourg and he became the leading reformer there. He had a huge influence on other reformers such as Calvin, Peter Martyr and several others.

What did his teaching consist of? Bucer (who lived from 1491 to 1551) was a key thinker on areas including the Eucharist, the split between Roman Catholics and Protestants and church discipline. For example, on the latter he came up with the idea of setting up small groups of élite Christians in congregations to set examples to the others.

His teaching on the Eucharist, one supposes, was what we now call Calvinistic? No. In those days the split was really between the Swiss and the Lutherans. He started off by reacting against the idea that the Eucharist was merely a symbol and so, in a move that was typical of him, he tried to mediate a path between the two extremes. So he taught a real feeding on Christ's body and blood, but without their real presence in the bread and wine.

Was he successful in that mediation? Far from it. Luther was, shall we say, less than impressed. But Bucer regarded himself as having a key role to play in church unity, only no one else quite shared that opinion.

He wasn't much of a diplomat then? That's one way of putting it. Someone has said of him that his approach amounted to 'an olive branch from a catapult'. But he rarely solved the disputes. At a church meeting in Regensburg, for example, he played a key role in finding common ground between Protestants and Roman Catholics on justification by faith. Agreement was reached, but again Luther was distinctly unimpressed.

What was wrong with it? Luther thought he had conceded too much ground, and spoke the oft quoted: 'Bucer stinks.'

Strong language. Yes it was, but lest you think that this man was a loose cannon, he was highly respected. In that debate both Calvin and Melanchthon agreed with him. He also wrote a book called *True Pastoral Care* that proved to be one of the most important works of the sixteenth century.

How deep was his influence on Calvin? He was really Calvin's mentor and would have had an even greater influence if the Emperor's army hadn't taken Strasbourg. That led Bucer and his wife (a former nun; he was a former monk) to move to Britain, where he took up a post as professor at Cambridge. Here he found a new outlet for his ideas, for he was a friend of Thomas Cranmer.

What sort of influence did he have there? He helped compile the 1549 and 1552 Prayer Books and wrote a book called the *Kingdom of Christ*. Edward VI was going to use this as the blueprint for a Christian England, but he died before he could implement it.

He must have died a saint. Perhaps so, but when Mary came to power she was so angry that she had his body exhumed and burned.

Least likely to say Once a Lutheran, always a Lutheran.

Most likely to say There are two sides to the coin.

RUDOLF BULTMANN

Vital statistics This German theologian lived from 1884 to 1976, and by the time he retired in 1951 he had made his mark on the Christian world for his Big Idea.

And what was that Big Idea? He was heavily into 'demythologizing' the New Testament, of which he was a scholar.

Sounds painful. Not really, his idea was that the Bible was full of myths, and while he adamantly claimed that he was only interpreting these (not eliminating myth) he still upset traditional theologians.

What sort of myths are we talking about? Not just giant fishes, our Rudi didn't have much time for any miracles, angels, demons or much else that was out of the ordinary. Of course, he didn't mean to imply that these myths were necessarily untrue, even if they probably were. He believed that they were just stories that may or may not communicate spiritual truths.

So what was left when he had finished with the New Testament? He thought that the gospel message could be more accessible if it were modernized and the language made more appropriate.

He was a busy man, then. Oh yes, but there's more.

He had other Big Ideas? He was quite enamored by the form criticism school of thought.

And what is that? This was a theology that examined the Bible and identified where its various strands were all likely to have come from. So, rather than accepting that Luke sat down and wrote his Gospel from scratch, they said part of it came from Q.

The guy in the James Bond movies? No, Q is believed to be the source (from the German word *Quelle*) from which Matthew and Luke compiled their Gospels. But Bultmann took it further and by the end there wasn't much of the New Testament that he believed to be reliable from a historical perspective.

So, not very popular with evangelicals or traditionalists? Well, you might be surprised to know that his efforts to make Christianity more accessible in the modern world are being taken up by both of those groups, even if his theology is still notoriously unacceptable to them.

Not to be confused with Rudolf the Red-Nosed Reindeer, Rudolf Hess, Rudolf Nureyev.

Don't mention Lazarus; the feeding of the 5,000; the resurrection.

Do mention Fantasy; conjuring tricks; form criticism.

Most likely to say It was sleight of hand.

Least likely to say I'm speechless!

John Bunyan

*T*he author of the Pilgrim's Progress? Correct. He wrote this, and some other books, while he was in prison, but it was this book that really caught the imagination of the wider world.

You say he was in prison. What crime did he commit? He had served early on in the English Civil War, on the side of the parliamentary army. When Charles II returned to the throne, times got hard for those who had not been faithful to the Church of England. As a Puritan, Bunyan was not, and he was imprisoned because he refused to stop preaching.

That sounds like a harsh punishment. It was, and he was in jail from 1660 until 1672 (and then again for a short time in 1677).

For such a well-known preacher, was there no public outcry? He wasn't that well known then and came from humble origins; born in 1628, his father was a brazier (or tinker). Charles II once asked John Owen, who was one of the leading intellects of the time, why he listened to this 'uneducated tinker'. Owen replied: 'Could I possess the tinker's abilities for preaching, please your majesty, I would gladly relinquish all my learning.'

So Charles had it in for him? Not exactly, but anyone who refused to honor the new Anglican Settlement was in trouble, and that included all of the Puritans.

How did a tinker get to be such an influential figure? Well, you know the old saying about 'behind every good man . . .'? It was his wife who set John Bunyan on the straight and narrow. He married in 1649 and his wife, who was from a godly family, introduced him to solid Christian books, but it wasn't until he joined an independent congregation in Bedford that he felt confident in his faith. He soon began preaching for his congregation, and it was this that led to his imprisonment.

And to the start of his writing career. Correct. His first book is thought to be *Grace Abounding to the Chief of Sinners*, which was published in 1666. This was an account of his own spiritual pilgrimage. But his most famous work was to appear much later, in 1678, ten years before he died and just as the persecution of dissenters was coming to an end.

Why did he write the Pilgrim's Progress *in such an allegorical style?* While the story of his own conversion would have been of limited interest, he believed that the world was the setting for a battle of spiritual warfare, and the only thing that mattered was finding salvation. So he wrote about the experiences of Pilgrim as he encountered the trials and temptations of this life. This reflected his own experiences. And it worked. His masterpiece has appealed to Christians from all backgrounds, and not just Puritans.

Most likely to say A good wife is a blessing.

Least likely to say Put me down as Church of England, mister prison guard.

Don't mention Charles II.

Do mention Pilgrims, preaching and independent congregations.

John Calvin

Appearance The Doctor of Geneva, and as you would expect of a sixteenth-century theologian (who lived from 1509 to 1564) he was famous for his long beard, gaunt features and stern expression.

Stern? Calvinism's hallmark, isn't it? Well, he was a dedicated gentleman– he was appointed to his first church position when he was just twelve. He then went to Paris where his developing views found a limited audience. He even pinned a sheet of these ideas (according to some) to the back of the royal bedchamber.

How did Their Royal Highnesses respond? We shall never know, but suffice it to say that it led to Calvin fleeing to Basle.

That would have been an early retirement. Far from it, while there he wrote the first version of his *Institutes*, which was to become his most famous and enduring work. In its final form it ran to twenty volumes.

So what's the Geneva connection? While he was passing through the city he was invited to stay on and help with the reformation there and did so. One of his big ideas was to use excommunication as a form of civil discipline, but a quarrel with the city council led to him fleeing from there too.

So his Geneva stay was short? After spending three years in Strasbourg, he came back with more big ideas: he wanted to see Geneva run as a theocracy, along the lines of Islamic regimes where the clergy write the rules for the whole of society. He was partly trying to focus on the problem of recalcitrant clergy, but he managed to get the powers to ban things like gambling and dancing, which he regarded as evils. But it was at this point that he advocated the theological ideas we know as TULIP.

So he was a gardener then? No, TULIP is a handy acronym for the 'five points' of Calvinism. Total depravity (which means that all are totally incapable of effecting their salvation); Unconditional election (God has known from the beginning who is going to be saved); Limited atonement (Christ died only for the elect); Irresistible grace (God's action in the unmerited forgiveness of sinners) and the Perseverance of the saints (God will not allow the elect to fall away from him).

Not to be confused with Calvin Klein, Calvin and Hobbes.

Most likely to say It's all explained in my book.

Least likely to say Save the last dance for me.

JOHN CHRYSOSTOM

*C*hris who? Not Chris, but John Chrysostom. Chrysostom was actually a nickname given to him two centuries after he died (which was in AD 407). It means 'golden mouthed', and he got the nickname because he was an outstanding preacher. In fact he became known as the greatest Christian preacher. Ever. No question about it.

When did he live? He was born around the year 347 in Antioch and he was brought up by his mother, who was tragically widowed when she was just 20. So he was part of a single-parent family. Because he was looking after his mother he was unable to achieve his ambition of entering a monastery. However, he followed the rule at home, and later became a hermit.

So did he start preaching at home? Not at home, but certainly in Antioch. He followed the Antiochian school that opposed allegory. They taught instead that the Bible should be interpreted according to its natural, or literal, sense. So Chrysostom, who was by now a priest, followed this and preached his way through whole books of the Bible.

And he became famous because of it? Yes, but he may have preferred not to have won this fame, because he was forced to become the bishop of Constantinople. He got the job because there was fierce competition for it and the powers that be wanted an outsider to stop the turmoil to fill the position.

How did he get along there? Not very well. If he had been a clever politician he might have fared better, but he was just a straightforward preacher. So when he started reforming the city and preaching about morals, the Empress took this personally and tried to have him sacked.

Did she succeed? Yes, and here the politics get very murky. It was all to do with the Tall Brothers.

45

Who? The Tall Brothers weren't an ancient folk group, they were a religious group who fled to Constantinople after the denunciation of Origenism. At this point the Patriarch of Alexandria (who was fuming that Constantinople had become a more important see than his) had Chrysostom tried on trumped-up theological charges. That was enough to have him exiled. However, his flock in Constantinople rose up in protest and the Empress turned white with fear. So she called him back. But it was only temporary and they secured his banishment a short while later.

What happened? Empress Eudoxia ordered him to stop carrying out his church duties, but he refused point blank. So while he was gathering up candidates for baptism she sent in the army. It has gone down in the history books that while he was being driven out, the baptismal waters were stained red with blood.

A sad end. It gets worse. When he was exiled his captors wanted him dead, but even though he was in poor health he wasn't dying quickly enough for them. So they deliberately killed him by walking him to death – they forced him to go on a long march on foot in bitter weather.

And didn't he decide the date of Christmas? Almost. The date of December 25 had already been in use, but when he was patriarch he introduced this date to the Church in the East, which had observed Christmas on January 6. And in contrast, he introduced Epiphany to the Church in the West.

Don't mention Empresses, Alexandria, Tall Brothers.

Do mention Christmas, preaching, golden mouths.

THOMAS CRANMER

Appearance A quiet, scholarly type who was summoned by Henry VIII to be archbishop of Canterbury.

Theology? He was probably Lutheran in his theology and while he was at Cambridge he met with other Reformation figures who held their get-togethers in the congenial surroundings of a pub in the city to discuss the latest thinking from the continent.

He became quite a famous archbishop? Possibly the most famous ever, thanks to his contribution to the Anglican prayer book.

But, not for giving Henry his divorces then? That was certainly part of the scenario. But Henry's real concern was less about his marital state than about the authority of the Pope in Rome to rule over ecclesiastical matters in England. This concern had long worried English monarchs. Cranmer, who became archbishop in 1533 (age forty-four), played a key role in overthrowing papal supremacy over the Church in England.

So he was a crusading reformer? More of a quiet reformer, actually. He was a godly man, sensitive and brave (as he needed to be) but he preferred reformation by gentle persuasion. Nevertheless, he was responsible for the Great Bible, the Litany of 1545, two Prayer Books and *The Reformation of Church Laws.* As well as that he wrote a defense of the doctrine of the sacrament and was largely responsible for the Articles of the Church of England.

With a record like that, he must have been highly regarded. He was, until Henry died in 1547. Under Edward VI he continued to reform church services into the vernacular and reformed the Mass into Communion. He was largely responsible for the abolition of the old style of church services and encouraged the trend of destroying High Church elements such as icons, relics and images in parishes. Despite all of this, he played little part in the dissolution of the monasteries, which was a big feature of the period. However, when Mary Tudor succeeded to the throne in 1553 Cranmer's days were numbered.

Why was she so upset? For two reasons: Cranmer got involved in a failed plot to put Lady Jane Grey on the throne and that, together with his opposition to the Pope, meant that the new Queen was determined to make him suffer.

Was it a bloody end? At first he was accused of high treason as Mary tried to turn the country back to Rome, but she spared his life. He was imprisoned and forced to sign many recantations. Those didn't save him though, and in 1556 he was burned at the stake.

In spite of his recantations? On the day of his death he renounced them and (according to Matthew Foxe) put his hand into the flames first saying: 'This hand hath offended.'

But his legacy lives on. Yes, in the words of the Book of Common Prayer which reflects his earlier Prayer Books, and in the scriptural spirituality which he pioneered. When Mary died the Elizabethan Settlement restored Cranmer's work.

Least likely to say Something in Latin.

Most likely to say Let us pray.

CYRIL OF ALEXANDRIA

So what was he famous for, then? Probably for leading the battle over the nature of Christ's humanity. But he was also something of a street fighter, in the days when monks would take up arms to fight their case in church councils.

Tell me more. The story began when he became a priest, thanks to his uncle Theophilus. When he succeeded Theophilus as Patriarch of Alexandria, his main concern was to counter Nestorianism.

What was that? Nestorius was Patriarch of Constantinople, and there was a big political battle between the two as to who was the most important in church life. But this battle was over the word *theotokos*, which means 'God-bearer'. Nestorius wanted to be orthodox, but it seems he could not accept that the human and divine natures of Christ were united in one person. He taught instead that it was Jesus the man who was born of Mary and thus is united with God the Word in purpose and will. Nestorius openly said: 'I could not call a baby two or three months old God.'

And Cyril objected. He wrote to him immediately and said: 'That anyone could doubt the right of the holy Virgin to be called the mother of God fills me with astonishment.' Some theologians have claimed that while Nestorius taught a 'pantomime horse' theory of the incarnation, Cyril maintained that the two natures of Christ were united in Jesus.

Was this a real difference, or just a confusion over words? The two positions could be summed up by saying that Nestorius believed in Jesus the man *and* God the Word – two different things – whereas Cyril taught that Jesus was the Word. So it was more than semantics.

What did Nestorius do next? Well, it was actually Cyril who acted next. He persuaded the bishop of Rome to call a council at Rome in the year 430 to hammer out the matter, and he got Nestorius condemned. The following year Cyril wanted to secure his success so he called a council at Ephesus, but he got fed up waiting for the bishops from Antioch to arrive, so he went ahead and succeeded in having Nestorius deposed. When the Antiochene bishops arrived they were furious and voted instead to have Cyril deposed.

And was he? At first yes, but he then made a deal with some of the more moderate Antiochene bishops and he was restored, but Nestorius was exiled and went off to Upper Egypt to die.

A sad end for the man. Yes, because in a book of his that was discovered in 1910 it is clear that he wanted to be orthodox and to affirm the unity of Christ, but mourns the fact that he was not successful.

And Cyril was hailed as the great hero. By some, yes. But his tactics were not universally applauded. He certainly did defend orthodoxy, and has had a great impact on theology since his day. But to get an idea of what others thought of him, read what Theodoret wrote as his obituary when he died in AD 444: 'At last and with difficulty the villain has gone . . . His survivors are indeed delighted at his departure. The dead, maybe, are sorry. There is some ground for alarm lest they should be so much annoyed at his company as to send him back to us.' He went on to ask the undertakers to lay a very big and heavy stone on his grave just in case!

Favorite word Theotokos.

Least favorite person Nestorius.

JOHN DUNS SCOTUS

Isn't he the one from whom we get the term 'Dunce'? Yes, he is indeed. This scholar lived from 1265 to 1308, but we know rather a lot about his views if not his life. And of course his name lives on in every classroom.

Was he really dull-witted? No, on the contrary, he was quite an intellectual. His main contribution to theology was to address the diverging strands of philosophy and theology. He tried to mediate between Aristotelianism and Augustinianism.

Wasn't Aristotle a Greek philosopher? Correct. When his writings were translated into Latin they rocked the Church. Scotus wrote rejecting Aristotle's view that the human intellect can only know things that it collects from the five senses, arguing instead that man has an intuitive knowledge – a sixth sense, if you like. He addressed many of the philosopher's views, and taught that if a creature existed then it must have been caused. If it had been caused to exist, then there must therefore be some agent able to cause it.

Sounds heavy. It was. You'll have to pay attention to this. Aristotle's heritage led to the growth of the Scholasticism movement at a time when people were beginning to regard learning as an end in itself, rather than as an aid to developing theology. Some monks, for it was they who were practically the only ones who were into learning during the Dark Ages, began to get into 'reason'. Some, like Anselm, saw this as a way of defining Christian doctrine, but it soon grew more widespread, thanks to lawyers.

Excuse me, lawyers? Yes, they started to use philosophical methods to arbitrate conflicts. When this practice found its way back to the Church people like Peter Abelard were condemned, but his followers, like Peter Lombard, developed it into a popular method of doing theology. And so Scholasticism was born.

What exactly was Scholasticism? An early method of applying logic to questions about ancient texts. (I told you to pay attention.) It became most popular during the sixteenth century. But even during the time of Scotus many theologians tried to hold to the older worldview. The popularity of Aristotle gave impetus to the movement.

And it was this reaction against Aristotle that led to his name being used as a nickname? It was, but he was no dunce, he was quite an important thinker.

So he was mainly a philosopher then? He was a theologian as well. He believed, for example, that the incarnation would have happened even without the fall. This grew out of his teaching that Christ was the supreme manifestation of God's love. Consequently, he also believed in the Immaculate Conception of the Blessed Virgin Mary. And he was one of the first theologians to teach this.

An original thinker? Yes, and for his efforts he was beatified in 1993.

Don't mention Dunce.

Do mention Augustine, Aquinas and Aristotle. (He could go on for hours about these.)

Jonathan Edwards

Surely you're not talking about the hop, skip and jump athlete? You're right, I'm not. This Jonathan Edwards, who was born in 1703, was an American evangelical preacher, and it was through him that the 'Great Awakening' spread across America.

What Great Awakening was this then? It took place in the 1740s. He had gone to Northampton, Massachusetts to succeed his grandfather as minister of the Congregational Church. But this was no nepotistic appointment. He was a child genius – he was fluent in Latin, Greek and Hebrew by the time he was thirteen. He went to study at Yale and then became a tutor there in 1724, when he was just twenty-one. Three years later he had a spiritual experience and it was then that he went to the Church.

Were they pleased with their new minister? You could say that he ruffled some feathers. His grandfather had reaped what he called 'five successive harvests' at the church, but Jonathan regarded his congregation as 'very insensible of the things of religion'. It may have been this that prompted his hellfire and brimstone sermons, but he clearly felt very deeply about religion in his own life.

Hellfire and brimstone? Oh yes, Jonathan had a way with words. In his famous sermon he said: 'The God that holds you over the pit of hell, much as one holds a spider or some loathsome insect over the fire, abhors you and is dreadfully provoked . . . You are ten thousand times more abominable in his eyes than the most hateful venomous serpent is in ours.'

Strong stuff. How did they respond? Things were different in those days. Rather than people suing for emotional distress, this sermon sparked off revival and was the beginning of the Great Awakening, which preceded the conversions of the Wesley brothers and George Whitefield. It even fed the Evangelical Revival in Britain.

He must have been a popular attraction at conferences. Perhaps, but not in his own church. He was rather strict and when he started to impose restrictions on who was allowed to take Communion, they discharged him. He then went off to be a missionary to the Indians.

Was he as successful in that? Yes, he wrote many of his greatest works during this time, and in 1757 he was invited to be president of the College of New Jersey (now Princeton) and reluctantly accepted. However, when he arrived the following year he was inoculated for smallpox, but died from the side effects.

How should we define his theology? He was a radical Calvinist and he vigorously opposed Arminianism. In one of his most famous books, *Freedom of the Will*, he taught that man really had no free will. He said that man was morally impotent: 'What he lacks is not the ability to do good, but the will or desire.' This fitted in with his Calvinistic doctrines of election, predestination and total depravity.

Don't mention Jacob Arminius, nominal churchgoers, thick headed liberals.

Do mention Damnation and suffering, revival, Calvin.

DESIDERIUS ERASMUS

Sounds like a Greek philosopher. You would be wrong. Desiderius Erasmus was a Dutch theologian of the Reformation period. Born in 1466 as the illegitimate son of a Dutch priest, he came under the influence of the Brethren of the Common Life. It seems that he didn't really want to go into the monastery, but once there his scholarly talents were recognized. He then got a dispensation from the monastery and became an itinerant scholar.

You say he was Dutch, did he complete his studies there? No, he came to Britain after spending time in Paris, but he didn't stay long in any one place. He went back to the continent in 1500 and turned down the offer of a professorship in Paris, devoting himself instead to the study of Greek.

Was his interest purely scholarly, then? No. He was a committed Christian and said: 'I would to God that a ploughman would sing a text of the Scripture at his plough and that the weaver would hum them to the tune of his shuttle.' He wanted the Scriptures translated into all languages ('the Scots and the Irish, the Turk and the Saracen').

Didn't Erasmus translate the Greek New Testament? Yes, and that is what he is most famous for. He was the first person to publish a Greek New Testament, although it was a rush job.

What was wrong with it? He heard that the Spanish were working on a Greek New Testament too, so he got straight to work. The problem was that he only had a few manuscripts to work from and only one had the Book of Revelation, and even that was missing the last six verses. Then there was the problem of the Johannine Comma.

Excuse me? The Johannine Comma appears in 1 John 5:7, 8 with reference to the Trinity. You can see it in the King James Version, which mentions the Father, Son and Holy Spirit, but in all other translations it is replaced by a colon and these words are missing. He used the words deliberately at first but later left them out, convinced that they weren't in the original texts. This caused many of his contemporaries to raise an eyebrow. And then, to add insult to injury, Erasmus published his Latin translation alongside the Greek. The traditionalists were fuming: the upstart had replaced the (official and highly regarded) Vulgate with his own version!

So his version was not popular? On the contrary, apart from the religious leaders, most others were delighted to have a Greek New Testament, it was the first time they had seen a printed one. This opened many up to the ideas of the Reformation. It has even been said that Erasmus laid the egg that Luther hatched.

Luther was one of his accomplices? No. The two had violent disagreements. The problem was that Erasmus liked the quiet life and he did not want upheaval, especially in the Church. However, he refrained from criticizing Luther when the latter was being attacked, and this helped him at a critical time. But he did write against Luther's idea that the human will is in bondage and unable to do any good. Unlike Luther, Erasmus believed that reformation of the Church could come through scholarship alone. He wanted a liberal Catholic Church and he believed that the way to achieve that end was to make people laugh rather than to wage war against the Pope.

Make people laugh? Yes, he was a bit of a satirist, a kind of medieval *Spitting Image* scriptwriter. One of his works poked fun at former Pope Julius II trying to get into heaven. He had a point in this strategy: one of the Pope's agents in Germany complained that his satires were more harmful to the Roman system than the Reformers. However, Erasmus was committed to the Church and this led him to keep his distance from the Reformers.

But the Pope didn't see the funny side? No, and when the Counter Reformation took place his works were banned by a dogmatic Catholicism. So at the end of his life, in 1536, he found himself stuck between a rock and a hard place. However, his legacy will live forever in his translation of the Greek New Testament.

Least likely to say The Vulgate is the only translation we need.

Most likely to say Mind your Ps, Qs and Johannine Commas.

FRANCIS OF ASSISI

He was, in a matter of speaking, a naturalist? Yes, but be careful not to confuse that with naturist, although it would be understandable if you were to see him in his youth.

What do you mean? Francis, who was born in 1182, lived a normal life for a youth of his period, but after visiting Assisi, prompted by a vision, he lost all taste for possessions. When he gave all he owned to the poor his father was furious and hauled him up before a court. Some say that he actually sold his father's possessions too, to give that money to the poor. In protest at his father he stripped naked and gave his father all the clothes he owned.

So he wasn't a materialist, then. No he certainly wasn't. This belief of his was inspired by the Lord's words in Matthew 10:7–19 and he wandered around in a long, dark garment. His empathy with mankind led to him embracing lepers long before modern-day charity figures got around to it.

Did this theology go over well with the Church? Not at first. After all, the Pope in his palace was understandably cautious about a man who wanted to sell everything and give it to the poor. However, Pope Honorius III eventually conceded to his way of thinking and approved his Rule of Life for the Franciscan Order.

He's popular now, was he popular then? His movement got off to a slow start, but he soon had twelve followers and later St Clare signed up and established her own order of Poor Clares. His vow of poverty may not have had widespread appeal, but his message did grow to be a worldwide movement.

Worldwide? Yes, he even went to Egypt where he tried (albeit unsuccessfully) to convert the Sultan to Christianity. But during his absence problems set in at Assisi and he had to come back to sort out the abuses.

So he established himself as the supreme leader? Far from it, he then went off to a hermitage having laid down his leadership. While there he received the 'stigmata' – five mysterious wounds on his body representing the wounds of Christ. He was the first person ever reported to have experienced this.

Was this a retreat to nature? No, he saw nature as pointing to the love of God and revelled in it, although he continued to carry out his work in the cities. He became famous for his concern for nature and it is said that even the birds and animals enjoyed listening to his sermons.

Least likely to say Is there a discount for cash?

Most likely to say Do you want the shirt off my back?

GREGORY OF NAZIANZUS

*W*asn't he one of the Cappadocian Fathers? Yes, most definitely, along with Basil of Caesarea and Basil's younger brother Gregory of Nyssa. The three of them are famous for their teaching on the Trinity, although they also opposed Arianism in the early Church. Gregory of Nazianzus (a city that is now in Turkey) was known as The Theologian and lived from around 329 to 390.

Were the three close friends? Yes, our Gregory was particularly friendly with Basil and the two of them met at the university of Athens, where they studied together. The two were to continue their association long after their student days. Gregory was from a church background, his father was bishop of Nazianzus; but Basil likewise was from a noble background, and was the leader in this relationship. After studying, Basil went off to live as a hermit, and Gregory followed him; but their life in the desert was to be short-lived. Basil was asked by his bishop to go and combat the Arians and Gregory was ordained priest unwillingly.

So the pair were split up. They were, and for Gregory his experiences were not happy ones. Around ten years after being ordained he was consecrated bishop, but he never took up his responsibilities – partly because he was unhappy about his post as a priest. Basil's encouragement to take up the bishop's job floundered, but Gregory did become the bishop at Constantinople, having made the Nicene faith the orthodoxy of the Church.

And how did that job go? Not very well either, it seems that Gregory was probably more suited to the life of a hermit than a church leader. Although he scored a particular success at Constantinople, he resigned the see before the year was out and it was back to Nazianzus for him.

What happened at the Council of Constantinople? The Gregories led the attack against heresy and they won. They had a creed agreed, which some theologians identify as the Nicene Creed and which is still used today.

What was the theological significance of the Cappadocian Fathers? They defended the Trinity, and Gregory of Nyssa wrote a book called *That There Are Not Three Gods*. They drew together two strands, the teaching that Father and Son are *homoousios* – in other words, that they are the same substance – with the teaching of Origen that Father, Son and Spirit are three 'hypostases', or beings. It was quite an achievement at the time and Basil argued it out by drawing a comparison between humanity and an individual human being. Of course it was much more complex than that, but they convinced many of their arguments.

So they liked Origen. They certainly did. Gregory and Basil worked together on a book called *Philocalia*, which was a compilation of the writings of Origen. So they knew their subject very well when they were working out this theology.

What else did they do? They also wrote against the Macedonians, who accepted the deity of the Son but argued that the Holy Spirit was not part of the Godhead. Gregory of Nazianzus was forceful in calling the Holy Spirit God.

Anything else? The third heresy that the Council of Constantinople rejected was Apollinarianism. This denied that Jesus had a human soul. It did not survive the attacks by the Cappadocian Fathers at the council.

Least likely to say I want a big office with a fashionable desk.

Most likely to say Arius got it wrong.

Not to be confused with Gregory of Nyssa.

GREGORY THE GREAT

And was he? Was he what? *Great?* Yes he was. He was an impressive guy, Gregory (who lived from 540 to 604). From a noble background, he was a Roman who gave up his wealth and administrative work to become a monk. He was to become the first Pope who had been a monk, but he was also great because he turned around a decaying situation in Rome and extended the realm of Christianity, trying to establish a Christian commonwealth.

An early effort at European Union? Yes it was. Rome was suffering because of the invasion of the German Lombards and there was also famine and plague. He negotiated peace with the Lombards and strengthened the churches in Spain and Gaul, defended the claims of Rome against Constantinople and even sent missionaries to England. He was what we would call a 'take-charge kind of guy'.

So we have a lot to thank him for. We certainly do. It is known that there were Christians here before — some British bishops attended the Synod of Arles in 314 — but it was in 597 that Gregory sent Augustine to Kent.

How did that come about? The Pope was very outward looking, and the story goes that one day he saw some attractive children in the slave market. He was told that they were 'Angli' from England, but he replied that they were not 'Angles', but 'Angels'. And so he sent Augustine on this mission.

But it was really Augustine who brought Christianity here. Yes it was, although some historians see Augustine as being somewhat unimaginative and instructed by Gregory on how to convert the Saxon pagans. Augustine was quite good at converting the heathen wherever he found them. But he wasn't so good at negotiating with the patriarch at Constantinople.

What happened there? Gregory wanted to uphold the primacy of the Roman see, and so he called on the patriarch of Constantinople to let him use the title of Oecumenical Patriarch. The patriarch wouldn't back down, so Gregory stopped using the title, rather than share it.

He was an interesting man. He certainly was, and he actively promoted monasticism, founding seven monasteries, and he developed a form of liturgical music, known as plainsong, that is still popular today. We know it as Gregorian Chant, and it has had a resurgence of popularity in recent years.

Least likely to say Constantinople is ideal for Christianity.

Most likely to say Let's send out a missionary.

GUSTAVO GUTIÉRREZ

He was a great Liberation Theologian, yes? He was the theologian who put Liberation Theology on the map. The movement grew out of the political climate of Latin America in the 1950s and 60s. Until then it was thought that the problems of the poor could be solved by development and aid from the richer countries. Many theologians there thought this solution was wrong. One of them was a young man who had been training to be a doctor. Gustavo Gutiérrez, who was born in Lima, Peru, in 1928, changed directions and became a priest instead.

He had been a medical student? Yes, that was where he started, but he then went on to study philosophy and psychology at Louvain, which was regarded as the most Vatican II-friendly institution. He then studied theology at Lyon before being ordained back in Lima and made professor of theology at the Catholic university there.

What did he and his colleagues think was the solution? They argued that the Bible taught socio-political liberation. Gutiérrez complained, for example, that the Church spiritualized passages in the Bible rendering them meaningless when it came to issues such as poverty. He wanted people to take the words of Jesus seriously and literally, and that meant taking political action.

That sounds a bit Marxist. It was — they saw much in Marxism that they could agree with — but the Church took a different position. While the Liberation Theologians defended political action in this way, they argued that if the Church remained neutral it was in fact supporting the status quo, hence it was not neutral at all. This thinking was also supported by other theologians, who would not have been classified as 'Liberation Theologians'. For example, it borrowed ideas from Moltmann and Rahner, but it claims to be uniquely Latin American.

What was Gutiérrez's main contribution? His book, *A Theology of Liberation* (1971, and 1973 for the English version) became the most important book on the subject. He surprised many conservatives with his serious approach to the Bible texts, but he also surprised them by saying that Liberation Theology was not just a new perspective, it was a new way of doing theology.

In what way? In the past, the Peruvian priest said, theology started with texts, now it had to start with the people. The Bible is then interpreted from a concrete situation rather than from an abstract theory. It is a 'critical reflection on historical praxis'. But this also meant that theology could no longer be universal. What was happening in his native Latin America would only be relevant there. Completely different answers might be found in other situations.

So how does Liberation Theology define itself then? That depends very much on who you talk to. Some place a great deal of stress on Marxist ideas, others very little. There is no one viewpoint on the subject, but Gutiérrez is regarded as the most important figure in the movement. Inherent, however, is the fact that each theologian and each situation must be viewed differently.

Was all this radically new? Not quite. It was the culmination of all that had been happening in theology from the end of the Second Vatican Council. A new sense of enthusiasm and excitement was sweeping through theology and this was the outworking of that. And of course, from Gutiérrez's point of view, he claimed that all this was not new at all, everything he was saying was to be found in the Bible.

Don't look for him In the servants' quarters.

Do look for him On the picket line.

ADOLF VON HARNACK

A*nother great German theologian?* Yes, although he was more of a church historian—some say the best of his era. Adolf von Harnack was born in 1851 and he followed in his father's footsteps, for his father was a professor of pastoral theology and had already written a major work on Luther's theology. Adolf continued to argue and assert that the Gospels presented a system of ethics that underlined the notion of the universal human brotherhood.

What was all that about? As you will soon see, he had radical ideas about the life of the Church, many of which he said grew out of his studies of the life of the early Church. The problem with the rest of us is that we are only aware of a tarnished history. One of his key ideas was that the real message of the gospel was that humanity was united by a common appreciation of right and wrong. The teachings of Jesus showed that, and no more and no less.

His was an academic career then? Yes, he started off lecturing at Leipzig and followed that up with Giessen, Marburg and Berlin. He made his name by studying the pre-Nicene period of church history and few of his peers knew it any better than he did. He also wrote about church history through the ages, but it was this earlier period that was important, for he argued that the truth of the early Church had been vandalized by the influence of Greek ideas, what he called Hellenization of the gospel. He thought we had fallen prey to metaphysics.

How did this go over? People were mixed. The conservatives were furious that he was questioning the Church's doctrine in this way and they tried, unsuccessfully, to stop his move to Berlin. He wanted to move the Church back to its early days, arguing that many aspects of modern church life were alien to the origins. He didn't like the creeds, the dogmas or even the sacraments of the Church, so it is little wonder that he made many enemies.

But did he have a point? Many scholars now share his opinion about the Hellenization of the gospel, but he was in the vanguard. Nevertheless, he also attracted opposition for questioning the Apostles' Creed, and this was a constant source of attack from his enemies. His critical attacks on doctrine, and indeed all aspects of modern church life, were to have a major influence on theologians from then on.

If he was a critical scholar were his ideas only popular with liberal theologians? Not all of his ideas. He surprised many people by going against the stream and advocating early dates for the Synoptic Gospels – Matthew, Mark and Luke. Many of his contemporaries were advocating late dates but Harnack even suggested an early date for 'Q' – the source document for some of those Gospel accounts. He also said that Acts was written at an early date by Luke, so his views cannot easily be categorized as liberal or otherwise.

What else did he write about? Gnosticism, Ignatius of Antioch and monasticism were three of the subjects, but he was also ennobled in his native Germany (hence the 'von' in his name) and he wrote a history of Berlin Academy. He achieved a great deal in his seventy-nine years.

Least likely to say Don't question the Church.

Most likely to say It's all Greek to me.

HILDA

A British saint? Yes indeed. Hilda lived from 614 to 680 and we know a lot about her, thanks to the Venerable Bede.

What did she do? She was actually a royal, descended from the Northumbrian royal line. Her sister, Hereswith, became a nun in France, and Hilda had set off to join her in nun's orders.

Did she take the vows? No, she got as far as East Anglia when she got the call.

From God? No, from Aidan, who wanted her to be abbess of a religious house near Hartlepool. And this she did.

Is this why she became a nun? Almost. In fact she soon went to Streanaeshalch to set up a monastery for men and women. And that is why she is so famous.

Famous? I've never heard of the place. And it's not surprising, for Streanaeshalch was later renamed Whitby.

So she got this sainthood for her monastery work? Partly. But also partly because of a church battle. You see at the time there were great struggles between the Celtic Christians and the Roman Christians. This had been going on since Augustine of Canterbury's day. Hilda originally sided with the Celts, but when the Romans finally won the day she changed sides and remained loyal.

So it nearly all failed for her. Yes, but she knew which side her monastery was buttered on and it all worked out in the end.

Not to be confused with Hilda Ogden, Hildegard, Hi-de-hi.

Most likely to say Yes, boss.

Least likely to say The Celts were right all along.

HILDEGARD OF BINGEN

Was she a mystic? She had mystical experiences, from an early age. But she was much more than that. Although she was from a noble family, she was brought up by a recluse, Jutta, who was abbess of the community at Disibodenberg in Germany. When Jutta died in 1136, Hildegard succeeded her at thirty-eight years old.

Disibodenberg? So why is she called Hildegard of Bingen? That came a little later. By 1152 she had moved her community to Rupertsberg, where she had a large house built. This was to be her base for many travels throughout the region, and she even established a daughter house in another part of Germany.

But she did have visions? Yes, these were very famous and thanks to Bernard of Clairvaux, who convinced the Pope (Eugenius III) to take them seriously, her fame spread around Europe.

What were these visions of? We know what these visions were about because she wrote them down, having won albeit cautious approval. She warned against vice and predicted imminent disaster. Her visions were unusual in that she included visual art in the reports of her visions. A bit like Billy Graham meets Damien Hirst. She wrote that she had these visions not when she was asleep, but when she was very much awake. She also denied that she was mad. That reassured some people. She said that her visions consisted of a light more brilliant than the sun and she called it 'the cloud of the living light'.

Did these win her a following? Oh yes. It wasn't long before people like the Emperor, bishops and kings were writing to her. She found that she was the latest craze, but she was also an influential figure for her other gifts.

What gifts? The diminutive Hildegard wrote an unusual book for her time called the *Book of Simple Medicine*. It was unusual in that she had a clear insight into medicine. Some say she also tried to concoct a cure for headaches. But she also wrote plays, music, poetry and drama. Some even claim that she was the first recorded woman in Europe who composed music. She was certainly multi-talented.

She must have been a celebrated figure in the Church. She was, largely. Apart from the situation with the Chapter of Mainz.

What happened there? She was something of an organizer, as we can see from her various works, but one thing she organized did not go over well with her superiors. That was when she tried to organize a strike by monks and nuns. For a short period her convent was placed under an interdict.

So she was an activist. Yes, we don't normally expect mystical types to organize pickets, but then Hildegard was never one to be easily categorized. She was a lover of nature, and argued that it be treated with respect. She was also an early advocate of equal rights, especially before God. She maintained that men and women were equal before God.

What was her main work? It was a book called *Scivias*, which is divided into three books with twenty-six of her visions. Then she wrote another work, *Liber vitae meritorium*, which contains six books. There was another one after that (*Liber divinorum operum*), and together with her letters these comprise a great quantity of material. What sets them apart, besides their content, is the lavish illustrations she produced herself.

A saint. Not at the time, and for a long time – two centuries, in fact – efforts to have her canonized floundered. Since the fifteenth century, however, she has been regarded as a saint.

Not to be confused with Hilda.

Most likely to say I'm not mad, really.

Least likely to say I dream in black and white.

RICHARD HOOKER

Sounds like a modern man. Well he isn't. He lived in 1554–1600 and was one of the key supporters of the Elizabethan Settlement in England.

Could you just refresh my memory on that? The Settlement was agreed just after the death of Queen Mary, when Elizabeth I took to the throne. You may recall that Mary tried to turn the Church back to Rome, but when she died different factions campaigned for change. On the Rome side many wanted the reforms that had been introduced to be reversed, but on the other side many wanted the Reformation to be enshrined in law.

And what side did Elizabeth take? She leaned more to the Rome side, but so many of the clergy and people fought against it that she had to compromise. The Settlement therefore was the absolute maximum that she would consider, but for the opponents, it marked the bare minimum of what they wanted.

So what was Hooker's role in all of this? Nothing. He was only five years old when it was agreed, but later he was to be one of the main supporters of it.

He agreed with it, then? Yes he did, but his support may have just been because it was the status quo. He was, after all, something of an establishment man. He wanted to defend it against the Puritans who took a very hard-line stance on these matters. They taught, for example, that only those things authorized in the Bible were permissible for Christians; Hooker thought that Christians should avoid only those things specifically outlawed in Scripture. If the Bible were silent on an issue, then Christians could interpret their stance according to their conscience.

Mr Hooker was a significant theologian? Yes. He started off as a grammar school lad in Exeter, before he went to Oxford, where he became a fellow.

He later married Joan Churchman of whom it was said, perhaps unkindly, that she brought him 'neither beauty nor portion', and he then resigned his fellowship. From there he became a rector and in 1588 became Master of the Temple.

This was to be his platform? Yes, but he had to share it. There was a reader at the church who preached in the evenings, and Hooker preached in the mornings. This highlighted the differences between the two men, as the reader, W. Travers, was a strong Calvinist. So it was said that in the mornings Canterbury was preached, and in the evenings, Geneva.

Did he write any books? His legacy to the Church is *Of the Laws of Ecclesiastical Polity*. Five of these books appeared in his lifetime, the other three posthumously.

So was he an all-round hero? No. Because he did not condemn the orders of the Protestants in Europe, he was accused of denying the importance of episcopal ordination. One church historian has said that one thing Hooker was not, was a Reformer. Others did not like his opposition to the campaign to stop clergy absenteeism.

What was that? It was a common practice for a feudal landlord to retain the tenured office as a benefice to a cleric (and therefore the income) and some priests would be appointed to a church benefice, but never actually go near them. Hooker probably thought these concerns were a bit too Puritanical.

Not to be confused with With an old-fashioned fishing vessel or a lady of the night.

Most likely to say How right you are, Your Majesty.

Least likely to say Dispose and unseat.

JAN HUS

A European theologian? Yes, he was a Czech national who lived from 1374 to 1415.

So what was he famous for? He was one of the first reformers and achieved fame as a martyr to the cause of church reform and Czech nationalism.

What were his concerns as a reformer? He stressed the importance of Scripture and elevated preaching to a high status. He was also concerned about sin and wanted to allow the laity to receive the cup as well as the bread at Communion. He had strong, biased feelings about spiritual pilgrimages which were popular at that time and he also was skeptical about priests forgiving sins.

But wasn't he a priest himself? Quite correct. He was a priest, but he spent much of his time teaching at the university in Prague. Nevertheless, he upset many other priests by preaching violent sermons against clergy immorality. His fellow priests were so incensed that they got Archbishop Sbinko to ban him from preaching (with backing from the Pope).

So that was the end of the story? On the contrary. There was a great split in the Church over two rival popes and Hus backed Alexander V as opposed to Gregory XII. He got royal endorsement and this helped him to promote the doctrines of his hero, John Wycliffe.

Victory is so sweet. But it was only temporary. Sbinko, isolated after the king supported Gregory XII, transferred his allegiance to Alexander and got him to agree to the destruction of all Wycliffe's books and even to ban preaching in private chapels. So Hus was stymied. And excommunicated.

And was he packed off to the ecclesiastical equivalent of Siberia? Well, he was kicked out of Prague, and he sought refuge with his supporters and spent his time writing. Diplomatic attempts were made at trying to find common ground but these foundered. He then was summoned to the Council of Constance and, assured of safe passage from the Emperor, set off. However, once he arrived at his trial he was thrown into prison and he died at the stake.

Strong stuff. Oh yes. The Inquisition, remember, had been active from the early thirteenth century and one pope, Urban V, was so mean that he even had some unbending cardinals tortured to death. So a little local problem like Hus (although together with Wycliffe representing the two most troublesome movements) was not going to concern the powers-that-were.

Was that the end of the story? Far from it. His death inspired his followers, who commemorated the date of his execution. The church that grew from that became widespread and inspired the Wesleys and the Evangelical Awakening in Britain. The Moravian Church is the descendant of Hus's church and the outward mission of the Church was one of their main priorities. It has been said that in the eighteenth century they achieved more than all the Protestant efforts before then.

Least likely to say I'm organizing a pilgrimage to Lourdes.

Most likely to say Clergy have to clean up their act.

IGNATIUS OF ANTIOCH

Was *he the one who invented the retreats?* No, the Ignatian retreats are named after Ignatius Loyola. This one is the original St Ignatius, who lived from AD 35 to 107. Not much is known about him, he really only comes to prominence as he is on his way to Rome, condemned to be 'devoured by wild beasts'.

And why was that journey important? Because on the way he wrote several letters that give us a clear insight to the Christian world of that time. Ignatius, who was bishop of Antioch, was the first Christian writer outside the Bible to stress the Virgin Birth and he was the first to talk about the 'Catholic' Church, meaning the universal Church. His letters also stress the pattern of bishops, presbyters and deacons in the structure of the Church.

So the pattern goes a long way back. It certainly does. It is thought that Ignatius was a disciple of the apostle John, and we also know that he was either the second bishop of Antioch (the first was Peter) or the third, depending on whether you prefer to listen to Origen or Eusebius. So he was close to the original disciples and an important figure.

Why was he being sent to Rome? During the rule of Trajan there was an outbreak of persecution and Ignatius was one of those condemned to death for their beliefs. On the way he wrote these letters to the churches at Ephesus, Magnesia, Tralles, Rome, Philadelphia and Smyrna, and one to Polycarp.

Do we still have these letters? We know that many quotations from them feature in other writings from the time, but there was confusion over whether some were genuine or not. Two camps emerged, those favoring the episcopacy who took them all as genuine due to their high view of the place of bishops, and those who were skeptical. However, the Irish bishop

James Ussher, in the eighteenth century, identified seven that he claimed were genuine. Some were not convinced, as he said that he found the original texts in England, but when a newly discovered Latin translation corroborated the findings, those seven were widely accepted as genuine.

So this is an early proof of the primacy of the bishop of Rome. Not quite. He doesn't actually refer to the bishop of Rome at all in these letters, and anyway some theologians point out that while he does talk about the place of the bishop, he doesn't really give credence to the monarchical style of bishop that we know today. So we can't draw too much from these letters.

What else was in the letters? He stressed church unity and he made a strong stand against heresy, in particular against Docetism.

Refresh my memory on that one. Docetism was the view that Jesus only seemed to be human, and that he only seemed to suffer on the cross. It was a popular heresy at the time and Ignatius was very strong in his condemnation of it. He was clear about Christ's humanity and his deity. He referred to Christ in his letters as 'our God Jesus Christ'. And he wrote about the flesh of Christ, 'the flesh that suffered for our sins'.

We know he was on the way to Rome, was he actually martyred there? Yes, the evidences are very strong. Origen states emphatically that Ignatius was martyred in the Coliseum there.

And he is a saint of the Church? He is indeed.

Not to be confused with Ignatius Loyola, Ignoramus.

Most likely word to use Catholic.

Least likely word to use Recant.

IRENAEUS

A *nother ancient theologian?* One of the most ancient. We know that
he learned his theology from Polycarp, who himself was a friend of
the apostle John, so he comes from a very early period in the life of the
Church.

When, exactly? He dates from around 130 to around 200. His life is a little hazy almost 2,000 years later, but it is thought, because of the Polycarp
connection, that he came from Smyrna. However, he didn't stay there very
long, as we know that he soon became a priest in Lyons, Gaul (present-day
France). He is important to us for many reasons, not least of which is that
he attacked the Gnostics

Who were they? That is a modern term for a group of people who were
heretics in that they believed salvation could be achieved through knowledge. They did not believe that Christ was really God, they denied that he
rose from the grave and they denied that the world was created by one
God. These Gnostics also had lots of various beliefs they claimed had been
handed on to them secretly by one or other of the apostles.

And Irenaeus begged to differ. He certainly did. He wrote five volumes of
works against them, called *Five Books Exposing and Overthrowing the So-
Called 'Knowledge'.*

Catchy title. We know it better as *Against Heresies.* Is that a bit upbeat?
Anyway, these books were, until the mid-nineteenth century, among the
few sources of information about these early beliefs. Books found then
confirmed and broadened our knowledge of what the Gnostics believed.
Irenaeus was quite firm in opposing them. In fact, he believed that one
way to ridicule them was to expose what they believed: for them it was
'secret' knowledge, he thought it was nonsense.

How did he convince them that he was right and they were wrong? They claimed to have received this secret knowledge from the apostles. But he claimed that he could trace the Church's teaching back to the original apostles, and argued that there was no break in what the first apostles taught with what he taught. Therefore he was right and they weren't.

How important was that? It was very important for the Church as it introduced the principle of apostolic succession. For Irenaeus it was monumentally important as it stopped the Gnostics claiming that their ideas were the correct interpretation of the life of Christ. For Irenaeus to claim that only Polycarp and John separated him from Christ gave him an ace to play when people said his theology was wrong.

And what else did he achieve? Irenaeus stated for the first time that the four Gospels we know (Matthew, Mark, Luke and John) were the only true ones. And he said that the writings of the New Testament were on the same level of authority as the Old Testament.

How did he do that? In his book *Proof of Apostolic Preaching* he taught that the Christian faith fulfilled what it said in the Old Testament, and therefore that the books of the New Testament were to be treated as Holy Scripture.

What was his theology? Very orthodox. He said that Christ did die and rise again, that he was fully God and fully human, he identified a 'Rule', which was basically a form of creed that summed up all of this. And he also taught that Christ summed up history. This he called the 'recapitulation'.

What did that mean? It meant that Christ had followed in the footsteps of Adam but that he reconciled the world to God rather than separating the two. Irenaeus broke new ground by comparing Mary to Eve, describing the mother of Jesus as the Second Eve, thus giving her a new and enhanced status in the Church's doctrine.

Least favorite people Gnostics.

Most favorite people Apostles.

JEROME

Didn't he translate the Bible? The main achievement of Jerome (around 345–420), who was a brilliant scholar, was to translate the Bible into Latin. He even spent twenty-three years learning Hebrew so that he could translate the Old Testament from the original rather than from the Greek version that was so prominent.

When did he do all of this? He was born early in the fourth century, but no one really knows quite when. Some think that he lived until his nineties but what we do know is that he was born in Italy and became a Christian when he was nineteen. He then opted for an ascetic lifestyle, and joined a monastery set up by Pachomius. However, a vision turned him away from his interest in academic studies and prompted him to go into the Church instead.

He became a priest. Yes, and he set off to study with Gregory of Nazianzus in Constantinople. He later got a job as secretary to the Pope, Damasus, in Rome and it was Damasus who urged him to start translating the Bible.

And did he start doing that immediately? No. The Pope soon died, leaving Jerome (real name: Sophronius Eusebius Hieronymus) without a job. He then set off to do some more travelling, going first to Antioch then Egypt before settling down in the Holy Land. He spent the next part of his life in Bethlehem, where he really got down to the job of translation.

When was that? We know that he began this work in 386, and it took him twenty-three years to complete his task. This became known as the Vulgate Bible ('Vulgate' meaning 'common use'). It remained the standard Bible of the Church for centuries, and is used even to the present day.

What made it so special? Until that time there were many translations of the Greek scriptures (including the Greek Old Testament, the Septuagint). However, few of these were particularly useful and Pope Damasus wanted a reliable translation to replace the corrupted versions in circulation. The need for such a translation was obvious, but Jerome did not just translate the Greek, he wanted to give his readers 'the hidden treasures of Hebrew erudition', and that was why he spent so long learning Hebrew.

And was his only work the translation? No, he advocated the Hebrew canon of the Old Testament, so criticizing the inclusion of the Apocrypha in the list of agreed books of the Old Testament. He also wrote many commentaries on the Bible, and he contributed to the debate on the disputed passages in John's Gospel.

What disputed passages? If you look in your Bible you might find that John 7:53—8:11 is marked in a different way from the other verses. This is because there was a question about whether these verses were in the original. Some manuscripts had them, others didn't. Jerome did include them (and Augustine seemed to know about them too). And the fact that he did has led to some dispute in the Church. Although we have to say that Jerome was not averse to a little dispute himself.

Why not? It seems that he was always falling out with people, and he could be petty, vicious and vindictive. A strange trait for one who once said: 'The friendship that can cease has never been real.' But his legacy has not been affected by the character blemish.

Did the Church recognize him for his work? If you have seen paintings of Jerome he probably had a red hat, suggesting that he was made a cardinal, but there is no proof of that. It might be like the lion myth.

What lion myth? In some of the paintings and statues of him, he is depicted with a lion at his feet. The story goes that he once removed a thorn from the foot of a lion and it thereafter helped him by recovering a stolen donkey. That, like the cardinal idea, may or may not be true.

Least likeable character trait Moodiness.

Most likeable character trait Commitment.

JOHN JEWEL

He *was one of the reformers, was he not?* Yes, and a very important person in the life and history of the Church of England.

How so? It was when he was at Oxford (Corpus Christi actually: he started at Merton and moved over) that he bumped into Peter Martyr. Now Peter Martyr was a keen Protestant and convinced John Jewel of the merits of the Protestant cause. Although Jewel put his name to a group of anti-Protestant articles in 1554, when he was thirty-two, he was still forced to flee by Queen Mary, who was not convinced that he really had given up his Protestant ways.

Where did he go? First of all he went to Strasbourg and then to Zurich, but even then he wasn't quite the Protestant that one would think. He opposed John Knox and some of the Calvinists over there. But when Mary died, he came back to Britain.

He was back in favor. And how. Queen Elizabeth took a shine to him and suggested that he train to be a bishop. He did and in 1560 he was consecrated bishop of Salisbury.

Was he still a Protestant? In a particularly Anglican way, yes. He held the middle ground between the Roman Catholics and the Puritans. He upset the Roman Catholics by writing the *Apologia Ecclesiae Anglicanae.*

What was in that? It was a powerful book, and it set the course for the Church of England ever since. He was essentially defending the Anglican Settlement but he went further. He argued that the Church of England was doctrinally sound because it could trace apostolic succession and claimed that unity was dependent on Christ, not the See of Rome, which he accused of having heretical doctrines.

And this was the 'middle ground'? It was at the time. On the opposing side were the Puritans, but the argument was really with the Roman Catholic authorities. The Church of England had to have a solid ground of defense for its existence outside the Roman fold. Jewel gave it this.

What was the Roman reaction? What do you think? He upset them by saying that a general reformation was required, but he also maintained that the Church was not capable of making even a single article of faith by itself, all the Church could do was to embrace Scripture. And he argued that when it came to church organization, every church had the right to do so through regional synods, without having to refer to Rome every time.

Quite an achievement for a diocesan bishop. Yes, he was not the archbishop of Canterbury, but he gave the Church of England a defense for its existence – that it was scriptural, wide-ranging and reasonable – that has stood the test of time.

And he influenced others with his work? Yes, and through his own patronage. He also paid for the welfare of many other 'poor boys' as part of his charitable work, and one of those he put through university was Richard Hooker, who was to carry on this work after Jewel died.

Most favorite phrase Via media.

JOHN OF DAMASCUS

I suppose he came from Damascus. Yes he did. His real name was John Mansour, although he was known by his birthplace. He was the last of the early Church 'Fathers', but we don't know a great deal about him. He was born in Damascus and came from a noble family. He lived probably sometime between 655 and 750 and is venerated by the Orthodox, partly for his defense of icons.

Was that controversial? Yes, and it still is in some parts of the Church. He maintained that icons were only a depiction of the reality and argued that Christians ought to venerate icons in the same way as we venerate the Bible or the cross. The supporters talked about these icons being 'written', rather than drawn, to emphasize their spiritual importance.

Did he convince many people? Yes he did. There was a prevailing adversion to icons, with the opponents known as 'iconoclasts' (image breakers). But when Constantine V's son took over, he was not an enthusiastic iconoclast, as his father was. After he died his widow, who was regent for their son, overturned the iconoclastic policy. But she had her sights set higher, and, with the support of people like John, got the Council of Nicaea to condemn the whole iconoclastic movement.

Was that the end of the matter? Not at all. An influential movement sprang up and eventually Emperor Leo V decided that iconoclasm should be the official policy of his government. This was bad news for supporters of icons, for key leaders were deposed, sent into exile or imprisoned. Later Emperor Theophilus actually decreed that the punishment for the icon supporters should be exile or capital punishment.

What happened next? Politics happened next. Theodora, the widow of Theophilus and regent for their son, decided that to secure the widest support for her offspring she should abandon the iconoclastic policy. And so it was. A synod in 843 condemned the iconoclasts, deposed the patriarch and made relations between the Byzantine government and the Orthodox Church more harmonious. Even today the Orthodox celebrate the first Sunday in Lent as the Feast of Orthodoxy, marking the end of the iconoclastic controversy.

And John's main contribution was on icons. It wasn't his main contribution, but it was important. He also wrote some important works, the most famous of which was *Fount of Knowledge.* John's main achievement was to gather together all the works of the early Fathers into a systematic manual.

What were his main ideas? His theology was characterized by a fully developed Mariology, teaching, for example, the divine maternity of Mary. He believed in the Real Presence, teaching that in the Eucharist the bread and wine are really changed into the Body and Blood of Jesus.

Famous quote 'I do not venerate matter but I venerate the Creator of matter, who for my sake has become material, who has been pleased to dwell in matter, and has through matter effected my salvation.' However, he resisted efforts to criticize icons and went on, 'for it was through matter that my salvation came to pass. Do not insult matter, for it is not without honor; nothing is without honor that God has made.'

JOHN OF THE CROSS

Appearance? Shoeless. This was, of course, the man who, with St Teresa of Avila, founded the Discalced Carmelites. 'Discalced', in case you were wondering, means 'shoeless'.

Background? He was born into a poor Spanish family in 1542 and went into the monastery at Medina del Campo. After studying theology at Salamanca he was ordained. It was then that he began to get dissatisfied.

Why? He thought his fellow priests were too relaxed about their calling and he even contemplated quitting to join the Carthusians. But it was Teresa who convinced him not to go down that path. She encouraged him instead to join with her in her efforts to reform the convents. So he joined in, widening the remit to include the monasteries too.

What happened next? He went with her to Valladolid, where he lived an extremely ascetic life in a hovel. This seemed to suit his temperament, but it was to be short-lived, for Teresa appointed him to the convent at Avila in 1572, the year after she returned there herself. However, church politics entered into the equation.

In what way? These two were set on reforming the institutions, but their goals were not shared by everyone. Their opponents – the Calced Carmelites – held a meeting in Italy in 1575 and that was the writing on the wall for John. He was promptly arrested and thrown in the dungeon at Toledo. It was probably during this time that he wrote some of his greatest works.

What did he write? John of the Cross is one of the leading mystics and poets of the age. His best known work, *The Dark Night of the Soul*, might have been written during this time. Many of his works survive to the present day.

So what happened to the movement then? There was a split between the two, and it wasn't just over whether they could wear shoes or not. Both John and Teresa wanted to reform the movement in a more ascetic direction, but the split seemed to settle things for a while. He was later appointed prior at Granada. But his views hadn't softened. When the vicar general of the Discalced Carmelites wanted to impose new rules on the order, among other things, John objected. He was soon to pay the price of that.

How so? By the middle of 1591 he found himself banished to Andalucia. And while that is a particularly beautiful part of the world, for John it was a disaster. He fell seriously ill and had died before the year was out.

And he was a poet too. Yes, apart from the poem mentioned above, he wrote several others and all of them underline the importance to him of the mystical. He shared that interest with Teresa, but the mystical ideas, which were widespread in the period, are seen throughout all of his writings. He wasn't given so much to having visions as to believing that the reality of God's presence can only be found through the expression of love, which happens beyond the realm of the senses. This search for pure love motivated many during this period.

Not to be confused with John Chrysostom, John Jewel, John of Damascus.

Most likely to say You have nothing to lose but your shoes.

JULIAN OF NORWICH

Was he an Anglican theologian? This is Mother Julian of Norwich. Probably so called because she was the anchoress of the church of that name in Norwich. She lived from around 1342 to 1413 and is one of the most important writers of the Middle Ages, as her devotional works have had a major influence on Christians ever since.

What did she write? Her main work was called either *Showings* or *Revelations of Divine Love*. There are two versions, the shorter one and the longer one. But they are both about the same thing.

And what was that? In May 1373 she was suffering from a heart attack when she had fifteen visions about the Passion of Christ, with another one the next day. These tell of the suffering of Christ on the cross and the triumph over sin. They have become spiritual classics, especially the piece about the hazelnut.

The hazelnut? Tell me more. She had a vision and she wrote this about it: 'Our Lord showed me a little thing, the quantity of a hazelnut, in the palm of my hand; and it was as round as a ball. I looked thereupon with the eye of my understanding and thought "What may this be?" And it was answered generally thus: "It is all that is made." I marvelled how it might last, for methought it might suddenly have fallen to naught for its littleness. And I was answered in my understanding: "It lasteth and ever shall last for that God loveth it." And so All-thing hath Being by the love of God. In this Little Thing I saw three properties. The first is that God made it, the second that God loveth it, the third that God keepeth it.'

So her image of the hazelnut caught the imagination. Around the world. There wasn't much going on at this time in the Middle Ages, Christianity was in the doldrums, but her vision brought some new life. That, and her feminist ideas.

She was a feminist? Sort of. She kept on referring to Christ as our Mother, but this was not completely surprising at the time, even if we find it novel. She saw a parallel between human motherhood and that of God's treatment of us. Both allow their children to hurt themselves, while making sure that nothing really serious happens. So, according to Mother Julian, God will make sure that we are looked after eternally.

Everything will be all right. Exactly, and that is one of her refrains. 'It is true that sin is the cause of all this pain; but all shall be well, and all shall be well, and all manner of things shall be well.'

So we can relax. Some theologians point out that she takes a relaxed view of sin, that it can never really harm us, that God will overcome all in the fullness of time.

But wasn't that the whole point of the incarnation? Yes, and she had very clear ideas about it. She saw the world separated into two realms, the sacred and the spiritual, or 'substance' and 'sensuality'. Both of these come together in the incarnation and so both are reconciled to God.

Least likely to say Down with feminism.

Most likely to say All will be well.

Søren Kierkegaard

Another foreign theologian. Yes, Søren Aabye Kierkegaard spent nearly all his life in his native Copenhagen and it was probably the fact that he wrote everything in Danish that meant his influence spread slowly, but spread it eventually did.

What's his story? He was born the youngest son of elderly parents, and to please his father he decided to train for the ministry. However, he changed his mind after reading theology and became a writer instead. It was around this time that he got engaged to Regina Olsen, but he soon decided that his mission as a writer was incompatible with being a family man, so he called the whole thing off and died a lonely young man.

That was a brief life. It was, he died in 1855 at the age of forty-two, but he had a major impact on the world of theology and philosophy. He also invented 'Existentialism'.

What was that? It depends who you ask: every existentialist will tell you something different, but for Søren it started as a reaction against the formalism of religion. He believed that the churches had devalued Christianity and said that it was almost impossible to be a real Christian in a 'Christian' society where everyone was regarded as being a Christian, whether they were or not.

He had a point. He certainly did. He believed that the Christian faith was a matter of personal belief and not just assenting to some facts. He accused the churches of 'destroying Christianity by expansion'. It was so widespread that it didn't mean anything when pagans were treated as Christians. For him faith was much more dangerous: when people take the risk of committing their life to their God.

That sounds very Christian, not existential. Well, he was appalled by superficial Christianity – or 'nominalism' – but some theologians think he went too far by making the faith into a subjective, personal thing. They point out that he dismissed the quest for the historical Jesus because God appeared there incognito, an idea picked up later by Barth. His denial of objective truths was a precursor of the postmodernism idea.

And was sin a personal thing too? There Kierkegaard had different ideas. He said rightly: 'Take away the alarmed conscience and you may close the churches and turn them into dancing-halls.' So he did see the reality of sin, perhaps drawing from his own unhappy life. But this was again a reaction against the Lutheran Church, which he saw as being too 'friendly' with God. For Søren there was a huge gulf between man and God and reducing the concept of sin was denying the Christian message.

You said he had an unhappy life. Combine his abortive career move, a failed engagement, his relationship with his father and his own melancholy, and you have some key ingredients for unhappiness. It is difficult to know if the melancholy was sparked off by these other events, but he was never the life and soul of the party.

What was his relationship with his father? It all started so well, his father wanted him to be a church minister and young Søren was initially happy to oblige. He said later that his father 'believed that Canaan itself lies on the other side of a theological degree'. However, it seems that the youthful Søren found out something about his father's personal life that didn't square with his religious beliefs and this left Søren confused. That was when he gave up the idea of being a clergyman . . .

Least likely to say Eat, drink and be merry.

Most likely to say Tomorrow we die.

MARTIN LUTHER KING, JR.

The American civil rights leader? Was he a theologian too? Yes, he most certainly was. He followed in the footsteps of his father and grandfather to be minister of Ebenezer Baptist Church in Atlanta, Georgia, where he was born in 1929. However, his real story begins later than that.

Tell me more . . . It was in 1955 when King was minister of Dexter Avenue Baptist Church in Montgomery, Alabama, that a certain woman, called Rosa Parks, thrust him into the spotlight.

Not another naughty vicar story, I hope. Far from it. Mrs Rosa Parks was seated quite happily on a bus one day, only she was seated in the 'whites only' section. When asked to move to the 'black section', she refused. This act of defiance shook the community, and her pastor, Martin Luther King, Jr., was propelled to international fame when he took up her case for social justice.

Did he win? Yes, he achieved desegregation of the buses and one commentator pointed out that he had achieved more for black civil rights in America than in the previous three centuries.

Very well, but this sounds like it has very little to do with theology. And there you are wrong. You see the key to Martin Luther King, Jr.'s message was his profound belief in the gospel. He was brought up in the black evangelical movement, and was influenced by the social gospel movement, not to mention the teachings of Mahatma Gandhi, but in this volatile situation he preached the power of Christian love over hate.

And the people paid attention? Yes they did. He went further than Gandhi by calling not just for the reconciliation of the white to the black, but of the black to the white also. His message was summed up in one of his most famous speeches: 'We shall match your capacity to inflict suffering with our capacity to endure suffering. We will meet your physical force with soul force. Do to us what you will and we shall still love you. Send your hooded perpetrators of violence into our community at the midnight hour and beat us and leave us half-dead, and we shall still love you. But be assured that we will wear you down by our capacity to suffer.'

And he applied his theological beliefs to the social setting? Yes. He believed that the gospel had the power to change not only the individual, but the whole of society. Of course, looking back we can say that he had an enormous impact, and legal discrimination is now outlawed, but there are still great gulfs in American society. He justifiably said: 'I have a dream that my four little children will one day live in a nation where they will not be judged by the color of their skin, but by the content of their character.'

Did he live to see that dream fulfilled? No. His message won him enemies in both the white and black communities and on April 4, 1968, a shot rang out in the Memphis sky. Martin Luther King Jr. was dead. 'I've been to the mountain top,' he said earlier, 'And I've looked over and I've seen the promised land. I'm not fearing any man. Mine eyes have seen the glory of the coming of the Lord.'

And that was the end of the story? No, not at all. He had been invited to speak at the World Council of Churches at their Uppsala Assembly, but in his place went James Baldwin, who gave a devastating attack on white oppression. That led to the WCC setting up its Program to Combat Racism, one of its most controversial initiatives, with some labeling it as Marxist.

Not to be confused with Martin Luther (although it's easily done) Stephen King (he gives nightmares, not dreams).

Most likely to say I had a great dream last night.

Least likely to say We blacks know our place.

JOHN KNOX

He was the famous Scottish Reformer, wasn't he? Yes, that's correct. He lived from 1513 to 1572 and was a big fan of Calvin, whom he met in Geneva. So much so that he said of Calvin's Geneva that it was 'the most perfect school of Christ that ever was in the earth since the days of the apostles'.

And he brought the Reformation to Scotland? Yes, but it was a hard struggle. Patrick Hamilton, a Lutheran, who paid for his beliefs by being burned at the stake, inspired him. Knox and George Wishart developed the Reforming trend. At first he was a preacher at St Andrews, but he was taken prisoner by the French and sent as a galley slave for two years. After that he came to England, where he was made chaplain to Edward VI.

He was well connected, then. Not quite. When Mary took to the throne he fled to Frankfurt, for he did not share the modern outlook concerning the role of women in leadership. He believed that government by women was contrary to the law of nature and to Divine Ordinance.

I guess Mary was displeased. Definitely. And when Knox tried to return to Scotland she banned him from travelling through England. His return journey took an extra year. Then, when Elizabeth took the throne he wrote a famous book called *The First Blast of the Trumpet against the Monstrous Regiment of Women*.

So was all this simply male bias, or was there a theological point? It was a theological point, most certainly. It was all to do with the teaching of headship in the New Testament, where Paul said he wouldn't allow a woman to be the head of a man, because Christ is head of the Church. Knox had a political and theological aim too. He was vehemently opposed to Catholicism and he believed that if he secured the Reformation in Scotland, and England remained Reformed, there would be created a united nation won for the gospel.

He didn't have much time for the Roman Catholics? Not a bit. He lashed out against the Papacy, the Mass and what he regarded as Catholic idolatry. When he became the leader of the Reforming party north of the border he set up a commission which banned all these things and even ruled that attendance at Mass was punishable by death.

No via media *there.* No, and Knox had a uncanny ability of making enemies. When he was in Frankfurt he was expelled as pastor to the English congregation there because of his strong opposition to ceremonial in worship. But he was nevertheless a holy and devout man and this propelled his theological views.

But he secured the Reformation in Scotland nevertheless? Well, he had an impressive pedigree: in England he had helped Cranmer with the 1552 Book of Common Prayer. Some years later he helped draft the Book of Discipline and the Book of Common Order. He also helped draw up the Scots Confession that was ratified by the Scottish Parliament. So he may have had his enemies, but he was also very influential.

A happy ending to the story. But it doesn't end there. He had another altercation, this time against Mary, Queen of Scots, until her flight to England. She clearly didn't like him either, but she was in awe of him. She once said: 'I fear John Knox's prayers more than any army of 10,000 men.'

So not a happy ending for her. No. After she was beaten in battle she was tried and imprisoned and eventually executed. But if Knox had a vision of a united nation, that was to come after the death of Elizabeth, for it was the son of Mary and Lord Darnley who united the two kingdoms as James VI of Scotland and James I of England.

And Knox got his Reformation. Yes he did, and Scotland today reflects his influence and perhaps his belief expressed in one of his quotes: 'A man with God is always in the majority.'

Don't mention Women in leadership.

Do mention Predestination, discipline.

Most likely to say When's the next boat to Scotland?

Least likely to say What time is Mass?

HANS KÜNG

*H*e is a Roman Catholic theologian, is he not? He is a Roman Catholic and he is a theologian, but he is not a Roman Catholic theologian.

Explain. Küng was highly influential in the preparations for the Second Vatican Council, indeed, he came to prominence after his doctoral thesis was published. This work, called *Justification: The Doctrine of Karl Barth and a Catholic Reflection*, won him fame and was the main topic of conversation at every theologian's meal table. In it Küng claimed that there was no irreconcilable difference between Barth's view and the teaching of the Council of Trent. This came as a great shock to many, including Barth, who was personally delighted that the Roman Catholic Church had come to agree with his view.

And had it? That was the great debating point. Some agreed with Küng, others were not so sure, but on the whole Küng won the day. The consensus grew that justification by faith alone was acceptable Catholic teaching, and so had ramifications for their relationships with the other churches.

So he was well liked. He couldn't have been more popular. The Pope (John) was so impressed that Küng (who was born in 1928) was made a theological adviser to the Second Vatican Council and many of his ideas came to fruition there.

So why is he not a Roman Catholic theologian? It seems that even at the time of Vatican II the Holy Office had already opened a file on Küng for his *Justification* book. They were not happy with some of what he was saying and they decided to keep an eye on him. He didn't disappoint them either. He then wrote a book criticizing the infallibility of the Pope. As you would expect, this went down like a lead balloon.

What did he say exactly? He argued that the doctrine of papal infallibility was indefensible. Indeed, he went so far as to say that the Church and even the Bible could not be treated as infallible. What he wanted instead was a new definition of infallibility, that the Church is 'indefectible' – that is, that God keeps her in the truth even among error. So even if the Church did make mistakes God would ultimately keep her in the truth.

Not a popular position to hold. And especially not during the centenary celebrations of the first definition of papal infallibility. That was the final straw. Proceedings against him started, and it looked bleak for Swiss-born Küng. Even his allies seemed to desert him, but things did not go according to plan for the Holy Office, now renamed the Congregation for the Doctrine of the Faith. It should have been a straightforward case for them, but things ground slowly to a halt. Nothing significant happened until 1979, under new Pope John Paul II, when they deemed Küng to be no longer a Catholic theologian. They did not ban him outright, for fear that they would create a martyr.

So was he stopped from teaching. No, and he wasn't excommunicated either. What did happen was that they put pressure on to remove him from his post as professor of Catholic theology at his university of Tübingen. Even there things backfired for the Congregation, for the German state simply created a new post especially for him.

Quite a turn-around for someone who was a theological adviser to the Vatican Council. Yes it was, but it was not just about papal infallibility. He also spoke out against priestly celibacy and against the Church's contraception stance.

And he kept his job at Tübingen. He did, but he moved on to other aspects of the religious agenda, particularly in the area of relations between Christianity and other faiths. His work has been widely welcomed in all parts of the Church and in many countries.

Least likely to say The Pope is infallible.

Most likely to say We can all agree on justification.

IGNATIUS LOYOLA

What is his claim to fame? Ignatius Loyola was the man who founded the Society of Jesus–better known as the Jesuits. Born around 1491 Inigo Lopez, as he was known, was a professional soldier until an unfortunate incident with a cannon ball led to his conversion to Christianity.

What happened? He was seriously injured in battle, and while recuperating in his hospital bed he turned to reading books about the life of Christ and the lives of the saints. This had an enormous impact on him and he hung up his sword, vowing to become a soldier of Christ instead.

Not literally a soldier? Well, he was dedicated to the military lifestyle, but he took vows of poverty and devoted his life to Christ. Like the knights of old he dedicated himself to the cross. Perhaps because he really was a knight of old. He found six other friends who shared his views and they joined him in his quest. However, because they were hindered from going to the Holy Land they went instead to Italy and it was there that they came to the attention of Pope Paul III.

He liked their ideas? He was a little hesitant at first, but in 1540 he constituted the new movement, adding a fourth vow to the traditional ones of poverty, chastity and obedience. This new vow was of absolute obedience to the Pope. Loyola said that if the Pope declared that which was white was black, they would hold that it was black too. He wanted his members to obey the Pope 'as a corpse'. It was a bit reminiscent of the words of the genie of the lamp in Aladdin, whose catch-phrase was 'To hear is to obey.' Loyola had exactly the same attitude.

So they were to be the Pope's army? Almost, they regarded themselves as a kind of medieval division of storm troopers or swat team, who would go anywhere, anytime, at the request of the Pope. He required that members of his Society be of robust health, handsome, intelligent and eloquent. Their three tasks were to be education, counteracting the Protestants and undertaking missionary expansion in new areas.

How did he train them? Loyola came up with a set of Spiritual Exercises, which are still used today and even beyond the Roman Catholic Church. These take place over four weeks and cover sin, Christ's kingship, his passion and his risen life. It took up to fifteen years to train members, twice as long as they said it took to train children in the faith.

They trained children? Not as members of the Society. You may recall that famous dictum: 'Give me a child until he is seven, and he will remain a Catholic the rest of his life.' That was the Jesuits.

So who were the enemies of the Jesuits? Heretics. Particularly the Protestants. His experiences after his war wound were similar to Luther's, but whereas Luther wanted to reform the Church from all the medieval practices, Loyola wanted to reinvigorate the Church by restoring them. So he was crucial in what we know as the Counter-Reformation, although it could also be called the Roman Reformation.

And this Counter-Reformation was successful? Yes, but not in England. And the French later didn't like them very much. So much so that they had the order disbanded in 1773, although it was restored in 1814.

Famous quote We must take care lest, by exalting the merit of faith, without adding any distinction of explanation, we furnish people with a pretext for relaxing in the practice of good works.

Don't mention Protestants, cannon balls.

Do mention Spiritual Exercises, worldwide domination.

MARTIN LUTHER

Wow, this theologian I know—he started the Reformation didn't he? Yes, in his native Germany, where he was born in 1483. Although he seems to have at first believed in Nominalism, that man plays some part in his own salvation, he soon came to believe in justification by faith alone.

Was that what his ninety-five theses were about? No, he posted these on the door of his university in Wittenburg in 1517 against the 'indulgences' – spiritual benefits people were supposed to get if they contributed to the rebuilding of St Peter's in Rome.

That wouldn't make him too popular then? Exactly. While they were not as sensational as one might expect, their impact was remarkable. He was tried in Rome for heresy in his absence and later he was called before a cardinal to recant.

And did he? You've heard the phrase 'Here I stand, I can do no other'. That was his motto. When the good cardinal called him in Luther got even more emphatic. By this time the upstart was even denying the primacy of the Pope and the infallibility of the general councils.

Was there anything else in his manifesto? Almost every Catholic practice was questioned: he was one of the first to attack the celibacy requirement for the clergy, he opposed Masses for the dead, he wanted to question the Pope on doctrine and, horror of horrors, he urged the princes of his native Germany to abolish their tributes to Rome. There wasn't a lot that he approved of.

So what did the authorities do to him? He was called to the Diet of Worms.

That sounds a nasty punishment. Did he have to eat them? No, the Diet of Worms was a sort of synod (or church council) in the German town of Worms. He was given the chance to recant but when he didn't he was put under the ban of the Empire.

So he was expelled? He went off and lived under a pseudonym, but his work continued and his fame spread. The use of the vernacular in liturgy and the public reading of the Bible all helped and soon the princes were allowed to organize national churches.

So it is a happy ending? Yes, the Diet of Augsburg established the doctrinal basis of the Lutheran church, although there were further differences of opinion with other Reformers.

And was this his main theological emphasis? No, not really. Later on he became fascinated by the idea of justification by faith, after reading Romans 1:17: 'The righteous will live by faith'. He was shocked and offended by the sale of indulgences but this was nothing compared to this new theological understanding.

Least favorite place Worms.

Most favorite place Wittenberg.

PHILIPP MELANCHTHON

*S*ounds like something you buy in a tropical fish store. No, we are talk-ing about Philipp Melanchthon, the German Reformer who lived from 1497 to 1560. He was Luther's best friend, but they later fell out over the doctrine of the 'real presence'. Melanchthon claimed that Luther (just before he died) had admitted to him that he had gone too far. It seems that Luther could not change his stance for fear that all of his work would be undermined. But this allegation from Melanchthon only earned him the title of Luther's betrayer.

Was that his real name? He was actually born Philipp Schwartzerdt, but his mother's uncle gave him this Greek version of the name that means 'black earth'. Which name would you have preferred?

You said he was a Reformer. Yes, after studying at Heidelberg and Tübingen he became professor of Greek at Wittenberg, where he influenced, and was influenced by, Luther. He was a formidable scholar, something of a child prodigy, and found himself at the head of the Reforming movement. His temperament was very different from Luther's: he was timid, moderate and conciliatory. He spent a lot of time trying to unite the Reformed and Roman Catholic Churches, but this too proved controversial.

He sounds extremely active for a shy, retiring type. He was also an influen-tial academic, and one of his key contributions was the writing of the Augsburg Confession.

What was that? It was the Lutheran confession of faith, and to avoid upsetting the Catholics, he made it as moderate as possible. It consists of two parts, twenty-one articles of Lutheran doctrines and a second part of seven articles concerning abuses that have been corrected in the Lutheran Church (such as not allowing people to take the cup at communion). It was at this point that Luther fell out with Melanchthon. While the

Reformer approved the first version, a revised version moved closer to Calvin on the real presence. The tenth article now stated that 'the body and blood of Christ are truly exhibited with the bread and wine to those partaking in the Lord's Supper'. Luther was unhappy, but said nothing. However the hard-core Lutherans now had it in for Philipp. His moderation was at odds with the mood of the time.

Did he write anything else I should know about? His most important work of theology was the *Commonplaces* (Loci communes). It started off as a commentary on the book of Romans, but was revised many times. He was trying to rescue theology from philosophical distortions and return it to a biblical base.

Did the Calvinists now regard him as one of their own? Not exactly. He did come closer to their stance on the subject of the real presence, but he was still somewhat skeptical. For a start he regarded penance (albeit in a revised form) as sound theology. Then he regarded Roman Catholic rituals as of no importance and said we shouldn't get too worked up about them. And finally he taught that Christians are not to rely on predestination for their salvation, they must act justly. The Calvinists didn't like the sound of any of this.

Not to be confused with Plankton.

Don't mention Luther's last words.

Do mention The Augsburg Confession.

Jürgen Moltmann

He influenced the Liberation Theology movement, didn't he? He did. That came primarily from his first book, *The Theology of Hope*. Published in 1965, it attempted to show how God was at work in history to achieve his goals. To this end the Church could also be a people of hope because it is the vanguard of a new humanity.

So salvation is here and now. And in the past too. He thought that Christ's death on the cross was a pivotal experience of human history, but it was meaningless without the resurrection. This resurrection, he said, was just the beginning of God's work at reshaping society. While salvation was always interpreted as being a future event, looking forward to heaven, Moltmann said that it had to have a present outworking too.

And this was welcomed by the Liberation Theologians. It was, but Moltmann saw it as far more profound than that. Theologically, Christ's suffering demonstrated that God was concerned with the world. Those theologians who said that God was remote and not connected with our lives were wrong. The fact that Jesus died on the cross showed that God identified with the hopeless, hence it was a theology of hope.

Who said God was not concerned with our world? There was strong support for the concept of the 'impassibility of God'. Moltmann opposed this.

That we couldn't get past God? Impassibility is a technical term that means that God is unchanging, but it also means that God cannot suffer. It was this aspect that Moltmann questioned. In his second major book, *The Crucified God*, he agreed that God was impassible, but said that he could change himself and that he could allow others to cause him to suffer. Neither of these compromised God's sovereignty. But Moltmann said that if God could not suffer we could not talk about him being a God of love.

And the God of love was involved in the suffering of his people. From the cross yes, but also in the struggle of the poor, downtrodden and abandoned as they struggle for liberation. Moltmann made this conclusion as he brought eschatology back into center stage.

What had the end-times got to do with it? The consensus until then was that the end-times were the culmination of everything, but he saw it differently. He saw it *very* differently: 'The eschatological is not one element of Christianity, but it is the medium of Christian faith as such, the key in which everything in it is set, the glow that suffuses everything here in the dawn of an expected new day . . .' So the Christian story was the promise of what was to come, the hope to which we could look forward. Inherent in that was the need to work towards that future now, hence liberation.

He was a significant theologian then? Very much so. Born in Germany (Hamburg, actually) in 1926 he spent three years in prisoner-of-war camps, only returning to Germany in 1948. After that he studied theology and became a pastor. He was appointed professor of systematic theology at Tübingen in 1967 and he remains there today. Over the years his books have made a huge impact on the Christian world, partly because he entered into dialogue with the Marxists. He saw areas of agreement, largely because of his belief in the cross. He saw Jesus identifying with those who challenged the status quo, and so could talk to the Marxists on a philosophical level.

And was he as influential with the churches? Apart from the Liberation Theologians, yes. His thinking has been warmly received by the World Council of Churches among others.

Least likely to say Let's settle for a quiet life.

Most likely to say We all need hope.

NESTORIUS

Who was he? He was a patriarch of Constantinople, although the question that divides theologians is whether he was actually a Nestorian or not.

What exactly was a Nestorian? To start at the beginning, Nestorius was a famous preacher from the school of Antioch (which was a group of influential theologians) before he was made bishop of Constantinople. The trouble all started when his chaplain Anastasius spoke out against the term *theotokos*, which means 'God-bearer'.

What was the significance of that? This term was widely used and was regarded as being thoroughly orthodox. It meant that Mary was the Mother of God. Nestorius disagreed. His famous comment was that 'God is not a baby two or three months old.' However, his comments alerted his enemies to the possibility that he could be a heretic himself.

In what way? The way Nestorius described it sounded like he was arguing that within the body of Christ there were two beings, a man and God. Indeed, he said: 'I hold the natures apart, but unite the worship.' However, he also spoke of the oneness of Christ.

So was this just a battle over words? It was rather more political than that. Nestorius (351–451) was patriarch of Constantinople; over in Alexandria the patriarch was Cyril. Nestorius made enemies by his harsh approach to Jews and heretics, but when he started listening to clergy that Cyril had thrown out, Cyril was furious. However, his days were numbered when he took in some Pelagian exiles from the West. The Pope in Rome was not happy with that either. Nestorius was isolated. Now, armed with evidence of heresy, they moved against him.

He was cornered? He was. Cyril claimed that Nestorius was an 'adoptionist' – believing that God had simply borrowed the body of Jesus. So a synod was held and Nestorius was asked to submit to twelve 'anathemas'. He responded by issuing twelve of his own, so it was decided that the matter would be settled by a council in Ephesus in 431.

Who won? Some Syrian bishops from Antioch were late in arriving, and before they had arrived Cyril got Nestorius deposed. When the Syrians eventually turned up they were angry and condemned Cyril. It all became ridiculous at this point. Just then some Roman delegates arrived and they now backed Cyril. At the conclusion Cyril won and Nestorius was sent off to exile in Egypt, where he died many years later.

And that was the end of that story? Not quite. Nestorius denied that he had said anything heretical and even pointed out that Cyril had used arguments from Apollinarius, who himself had denied the complete humanity of Christ. So from his exile he wrote a response, under the pseudonym of the Bazaar of Heraclides. He tried to defend his views and attack Cyril in this document.

And scholars are still unsure about whether or not he was a heretic? Yes, many are. It is true that he appeared to say that Christ consisted of two wills, but he did also stress the unity of Christ. He did not deny Christ's deity but he was less explicit than he could have been about how the human and divine united. Some scholars accuse him of failing to combine the two to produce the Christ of the Gospels, but he never claimed that there were two 'sons'. Nevertheless, his term was 'conjunction' rather than 'union'.

And there are still Nestorian churches today. There is a Church called the Nestorian Church, but this dates back to the Antiochian days, and the doctrine of that Church has never been Nestorian in the way that Cyril would have defined it. You can find them in Kurdistan, Iraq and India.

Least likely to say Christ is God's son.

Most likely to say I'm not a heretic.

John Henry Newman

He was an Anglican who became a Roman Catholic. Yes, he was. John Henry Newman (1801–90) was sent by his evangelical father to a private school in Ealing, West London, before going on to Oxford. But it was at Ealing that he had a conversion experience, thanks to one of his teachers. However, commentators say that he was never a typical evangelical.

When did he go into the Church? He was ordained in 1824 and four years later he was made vicar of St Mary's, Oxford. It was around that time that he met up with some friends who succeeded in changing his attitude to the Roman Catholic Church and the Reformation. He now liked the former and disliked the latter. He became the leader of the new Oxford Movement.

What was that? Some people called them Tractarians because of their publication of *Tracts of our Times*, a series of publications that celebrated the Anglo-Catholic wing of the Church. He argued at first that the Church of England was the *via media* – middle way – between the Protestants and the Romans. However when one of Newman's tracts, *Number 90* (he wrote twenty-four of the series), said that Roman Catholics could agree to the thirty-nine Articles, there was an outcry. His boss, the bishop of Oxford, then banned him from writing any more.

What was wrong with that? Nothing with that, but he started to argue that the 'middle way' idea was wrong. He began to call the Church of England 'our stepmother', and it was this that at once indicated his movement towards Rome and the Church of England's distance from him.

And did he obey the ban on writing? Well, he was pretty upset by the Protestant direction of the Church and in 1843, two years after he wrote *Tract 90*, he resigned his cleric benefice, preaching a famous sermon called 'The parting of friends'. In 1845 he was received into the Roman Catholic Church.

Was he warmly welcomed? Yes, he was immediately made head of the Oratory of St Philip Neri in Birmingham, then was made rector of a new Catholic university in Dublin, so they certainly made something of their high profile convert.

But what was the reaction when he changed his theology so much? Soon after he was received into the Roman Church he published his Essay on the Development of Christian Doctrine, which was a defense of his new way of thinking. But he was still a little cautious on the role of the Pope and he was opposed to the wide-ranging powers of the papacy.

Did he get rebuked for that? No, undaunted, he went further. In 1875 he wrote a famous *Letter to the Duke of Norfolk* pointing out the dangers of the doctrine of papal infallibility. It didn't seem to do him too much harm for in 1879 Pope Leo XIII made him a cardinal.

Sounds like he was a very successful Catholic. Not so much at the time. A great deal of his work came to nothing, but his reputation continued to increase in stature after his death. Some point out that many of his ideas, such as biblical inspiration, the freedom of conscience and the role of the bishops in defining church doctrine, all came to fruition at the Second Vatican Council. Not bad for a young fellow from Ealing.

Didn't he also write a famous opera? It was a poem actually. It was in 1865 that he wrote the *Dream of Gerontius*, which, in a wonderful way, tells the story of the journey that begins at death. It was later set to music by Elgar.

A very talented man. And he might be a saint one day. He was declared 'Venerable' in 1991, so you never know . . .

Most likely to say All roads lead to Rome.

REINHOLD NIEBUHR

nother amazing German theologian? This time you'd be wrong. Although his father was a German immigrant (and Lutheran pastor) Reinhold was very much American. He spent a great deal of his ministry in Detroit and eventually came head-to-head with Henry Ford.

Why? Ford brought great attention to the fact that he was paying his employees $5 an hour, but when he unveiled his new car in 1927, Niebuhr complained about the human cost to the Ford employees, many of whom, he said, had been laid off for a year with no cash. This sort of approach was typical because of the politics and theology of Niebuhr.

Tell me more. He was an advocate of 'Christian realism' and in this he followed in the footsteps of Karl Barth and Emil Brunner. However, Niebuhr went further and said that Christianity had to be relevant to everyday situations. He was also famous because he spoke about original sin, a doctrine that had fallen out of favor among theologians and philosophers alike.

Why had it fallen out of favor? Optimism. Many people believed that with education the world would improve and there would be no need for 'religious' answers. The universities could answer all our moral problems. The Yale-educated Niebuhr, from his own experiences as a pastor in a working-class area of Detroit, could see through that. He even went so far as to advocate some aspects of Marxism, although he said that Marxism, as the answer to capitalism, 'has turned out to be worse than the disease it was meant to cure'.

And he said all this while a pastor? No. After his ordination in 1915 he became pastor of the Bethel evangelical church in Detroit, where he remained for thirteen years. But in 1928, the year after his run-in with Henry Ford, he was appointed professor of applied Christianity at Union

Theological Seminary in New York City. He remained there until he retired in 1960.

So his liberal views could not have affected his prospects too badly. Indeed, there was a strong movement against communism in the USA at this time, but although he could see some good points in Marxism he never quite advocated it. He never minced his words, however. He said once: 'Man's capacity for justice makes democracy possible, but man's inclination to injustice makes democracy necessary.' All of this grew out of his theological beliefs and can explain why he was a believer in the existence of original sin.

Is he famous for anything else? If you had ever been to a meeting of Alcoholics Anonymous you would be well aware of the words of Reinhold Niebuhr. He wrote a famous prayer that is used by Alcoholics Anonymous to this day: 'God grant me the grace to accept with serenity the things I cannot change, courage to change the things I can, and wisdom to know the difference.'

Not to be confused with His brother Helmut, who was also a theologian and was famous for the books *The Meaning of Revelation* and *Christ and Culture*. Although Helmut was younger than Reinhold, Reinhold outlived him, dying in 1971.

Least favorite person Henry Ford.

Most likely to say We might be lefties, but we're not commies.

ORIGEN

nother church father? He was a leading thinker in the early Church and was widely popular, but despite the fact that he was extremely influential, he was later condemned as a heretic. Nevertheless, his reputation was so great prior to that that it survived this calamity.

Why was he condemned? To understand that you have to examine his life story a little. Origen lived from around 185 to 254. He was brought up in a devout Christian family in Alexandria. His father was martyred when Origen was only seventeen and it is said that he was hoping to be martyred himself, the only problem was that his mother hid his clothes and this prevented him from going out and finding himself in an early grave.

So he was a young Christian. Yes, and after this episode he devoted himself to teaching the faith. He eventually got a job from Demetrius, bishop of Alexandria, heading up the catechetical school. This was an important move and his fame spread widely. He was soon travelling all over the world speaking and preaching in front of important people. And that was when the trouble started.

What trouble? He fell out with Demetrius and moved to Palestine. He had already been there once and he was highly regarded there. When the local bishops decided that they would ordain him to the priesthood, they forgot to ask Demetrius for permission. When he found out about it he was less than impressed.

What did he do? He sacked him and defrocked him. But this was not an important issue for Origen. This, after all, was the same man who lived such an ascetic life that he actually castrated himself, in obedience to Matthew 19:12. Origen then went to Caesarea, where he set up his own school, and this soon became famous around the world.

What did he teach? He taught much that was rather strange alongside that which was orthodox. Among the orthodox teachings he defended the Trinity. He opposed monarchianism, which taught that the Father *is* the Son. He also taught that the Son was eternally begotten.

What was not orthodox? He had this strange idea that everything was created eternally and that as these eternal souls moved away from God they became cold and hard. Eventually this caused them to fall, and some fell to be angels, others demons and still others to be humans, depending on how far they fell. Salvation is the reversal of this and Origen believed that at the conclusion of history everything and everyone would be reconciled to God, even the devil. This brand of universalism was denounced by the Church.

Any other strange ideas? Yes. He believed that evil was non-being, that punishment was psychological anguish, that the Son was inferior to the Father (and so we should pray to the Father through the Son).

Did he get all this from the Bible? Not all of it. He has been accused of importing thinking from the Greek philosopher Plato to biblical studies, and there is evidence of that. In his approach to the Bible he saw three levels of understanding: the first was the plain literal sense; the second was the moral application; the third was an allegorical sense. He was particularly fond of the allegorical sense, and his ideas about creation and the fall of man owe a great deal to this.

So was he completely off the wall? No. He wrote many serious works, one of which was called *First Principles*. This is believed to be the first attempt ever to do systematic theology, and he organized a system covering God, Christ, the Holy Spirit, creation, the soul, free will, salvation and the Scriptures. He definitely wanted to be orthodox.

Any other works I should know about? His main work was the *Hexapla*. This put in separate columns the Old Testament in Hebrew (he was one of the few scholars of his time to bother to learn Hebrew), a Greek transliteration, various other Greek translations and the Septuagint. He also wrote a book tackling pagan attacks on Christianity. Origen wrote books that were so long and complex that we only have fragments left now, but they are nevertheless very important.

Most likely to say We'll all be united in the end.

WOLFHART PANNENBERG

Sounds like another German theologian. Yes, although he was born (in 1928) in Stettin, which is now in Poland. But he is a great German theologian and is now a professor of theology at Munich University. He was a student of Barth, but he later distanced himself from Barth's 'revelational positivism'.

What on earth was that? It was Barth's belief that Christian truth is understood by revelation, in other words it is only for those who believe. If you don't believe then you won't understand the message of the gospel. Pannenberg disagreed. He said that the Christian message had to be logical and credible and could be understood by anyone, whether they believed or not.

So he made the case for a literal understanding of the gospel story? More of a historical understanding. Many of his contemporaries were teaching that the historical Jesus was unimportant, what really mattered was the spiritual significance of his life. Pannenberg objected. He said that this made Christianity an exclusive subject removed from the rest of the world. What he wanted was for Christianity to make its case in relation to every other academic discipline, and he was confident that the truth of Christianity could be argued coherently.

And how could he do that? In his book *Revelation as History* he made the case that the life of Jesus, and in particular his resurrection, could be proved and that faith came from looking at the facts, and not the other way around.

He took a different perspective? Yes, and he did the same in his Christology. He said there were two ways of looking at Christ, one was from 'above', and the other was from 'below'. The first looks at Christ as God and tries to comprehend how he became man. Pannenberg dismissed this because it took for granted his divinity. Much more interesting was the Christology from 'below'.

And what was that? This was looking at the life of Jesus of Nazareth and asking how he could have been God. For him the proof of his deity is to be found in the resurrection. He made a powerful case for this.

Did he convince his opponents? Not all of them. He did, after all, clash with them in a dramatic way. And perhaps his most significant contribution has been to make a case for historical credence and demonstrate that the resurrection can be grounds for faith, rather than arguing that one has to have a lot of faith to believe in it in the first place.

Has he been prolific in making this case? Yes, he has written many books, including *Revelation as History* (1961), where he first made his case for a credible Christianity. In 1964 he published the important book *Jesus – God and Man*, in which he claimed that the study of history could provide evidence for the divinity of Jesus. He developed a theology of hope with the central idea of God as the all-powerful force of the future. He has a particular interest in the future and sees God as the only hope.

Least likely to say History is nonsense.

Most likely to say What revelation are you talking about?

BLAISE PASCAL

He was a thinker, was he not? You are thinking of his most famous work, *Pensées* (Thoughts). And he was indeed a thinker, but he also played a major part in the life of the Church in the time of the Reformation.

Was he French, with a book title like that? Yes, he was born in Clermont-Ferrand in France in 1623. When his mother died when he was just four years old, his father gave him a private education. But from an early age he displayed an astounding intelligence.

A child prodigy? Yes, but this was not a misplaced talent, he went on to invent the calculator, the theory of probability, a law of physics (which made possible all of today's hydraulic equipment), the first wristwatch and he even set up the first bus route in Paris.

He was a busy young man. He was indeed, because he achieved all of this in a short life: he was to die when he was only thirty-nine. But he was also a philosopher, writer and religious thinker.

When did he write Pensées? Actually, he didn't. At least not as a book. He had intended to write a book called *Apology for the Christian Religion*, but because he died before it was completed, his notes (often written on scraps of paper) were published as *Pensées*. It put the case for Christianity against the rationalism of the day.

When did he become a Christian? He first talked about his conversion when he was twenty-three but it was in 1654 (November 23, to be precise) that he said his 'definitive conversion' took place. He then talked about discovering the 'God of Abraham, the God of Isaac, the God of Jacob, and not of the philosophers and men of science'. He wrote about this experience and even had the account stitched into his clothing, it had made such an impact on him.

So he didn't like the philosophers? He introduced a new way of thinking. Most held to an abstract view of the world, but he concentrated on fact and objectivity. So he said that if you were talking about knowing God, experience had to play a larger part than metaphysical speculation.

Didn't he make some statement about betting? More of a wager, actually. One of his most famous arguments was that if we couldn't definitively know if there is a God, we must take a wager on it, but with God rather than with a bookmaker. So, if we are wrong and there is no God, then the only thing we have lost in this life is sin, but we have gained a virtuous character. If we are right then we have lost nothing and gained an eternity of happiness. So there is really only one option a prudent gambler should take.

The Church must have been very grateful to have such an important thinker. He also had enemies. He didn't like the Jesuits and savagely ridiculed their idea of 'probabilism'.

What was that? It was an attempt to be kind to sinners. Basically it said that if one reputable authority (a Jesuit) said that something wasn't a sin, then others had to be lenient. But Pascal thought this meant that they were making light of sin and he made fun of them.

Famous quote Men never do evil so completely and cheerfully as when they do it from religious conviction.

Do mention Reason, computers, bus routes.

Don't mention Jesuits, Voltaire, stupid gamblers.

PELAGIUS

Who was he? He was a teacher, not a priest, who lived from 360 to 420 and was British in origin, although he spent most of his life abroad. He is an important figure in doctrinal circles, for he and Augustine battled over the question of grace versus free will.

What was the question? Augustine taught that man had no part to play in his salvation, it was all down to God's grace. Pelagius concurred. He had seen the lax moral standards of Roman Christians when he went there in 390 and so started preaching strict asceticism. He taught instead that everyone was created by God with the power to do good or evil, original sin didn't enter into it. Because of that it was important to live a holy life, and this was what he preached and practised. He believed that the only problem with people was that they were set a bad example, so he was going to set a good example.

He denied original sin. Some say this aspect to Pelagianism was added by his followers, of which he soon had many. The most important of his followers was Celestius, who is believed to have been an Irish-Scot. (His name is the Greek form of the Celtic 'Morgan', meaning 'sea-born'.) The two of them went from Italy to Africa, where they had their run-ins with Augustine. Pelagius himself went on to Palestine.

Was that when the trouble started? Celestius was the first to experience hostility, and it was over the question of original sin. He found himself condemned at the church council in Carthage, so he then left for Ephesus. That was in 411 and it was also when Augustine started to take notice of the content of their message. Pelagius was arguing that real grace was something that every person had and that it included free will, reason and conscience. To Augustine this was the very opposite of what was taught in the Gospels.

So he challenged them? He certainly did.

And Augustine won this battle? Yes, but not as quickly as you might suppose. In fact, early on Augustine treated Pelagius with a great deal of respect and it was only later, in 415, that things changed. Augustine tried to have Pelagius branded a heretic, but two councils cleared him. The African bishops took matters into their own hands and themselves condemned Pelagius and Celestius, and then put pressure on the Pope to have them thrown out of the Church. Celestius then pulled off a remarkable coup. He went to Rome to see Innocent I's successor and he talked him into reopening the case.

How did Augustine respond to that? He and his fellow African bishops stood their ground and issued no less than nine canons to condemn Pelagius and Celestius. And just to make sure, they got the Emperor to issue a decree denouncing them as heretics too. Faced with all of that, the Pope acquiesced and upheld the earlier ruling. Pelagius and Celestius were excommunicated and that is the last we hear of Pelagius.

But his influence lives on. It certainly does. As soon as Pope Zosimus had made his ruling, the theological dispute continued. One of their followers, Julian of Eclanum, continued the debate with Augustine. Celestius carried on the battle even without his mentor. He appealed to the new Pope, Celestine I, but in 431 the Council of Ephesus condemned them. From then on Augustine's doctrine was the orthodoxy.

But the issue didn't go away. No, it rumbled on throughout the Middle Ages and was even one of the issues debated during the Reformation. And since then philosophers as well as theologians have argued over the question of grace versus free will.

Least likely to say We all need salvation.

Most likely to say We just need a good example.

POLYCARP

When did he live? Very early in the life of the Church. His dates are usually given as 69–155, but Irenaeus, his own disciple, said that he knew the apostle John and others of the original disciples. So he is a link between the time of Christ and the early Church. It is possible that he was actually a disciple of John and knew the other disciples of Christ because of that. It is due to this that he is known as one of the 'Apostolic Fathers'.

What did he do? He was bishop of Smyrna (now known as Izmir in Turkey) and was extremely well connected. As well as knowing many of those who had seen Christ, he also knew Ignatius, another important figure in the early Church. One of Ignatius's letters to Polycarp is still in existence and is highly treasured.

Did he write anything himself? He did write a letter to the church at Philippi, and that has survived too. Perhaps one of his most important legacies to the Church is his opinion on the dating of Easter. Even at this early stage it was a much-debated matter and Polycarp went to Rome to see the bishop, Anicetus, to discuss the matter.

What did Polycarp want? He wanted the Church to follow his own 'Quartodeciman' practice in the Eastern churches. This tradition, which is thought to have gone back to John the Apostle, would have meant that Easter would have been observed on the fourteenth day of the Jewish month Nisan, whatever the day of the week, in line with the Jewish practice of Passover. The reasoning was that Easter was the Christian Passover. So Polycarp discussed this with the bishop of Rome, but he declined to join in. Nevertheless, he had no problems with the Eastern Churches carrying on with their own practice. It was many years later that the then bishop of Rome, Victor, tried to stamp out the Eastern practice and bring them into line.

And what happened next to Polycarp? It all took a turn for the worse. He had only just got back to Smyrna when there was an uprising and he was arrested. It was nothing less than mob rule and the Roman governor tried to let him off the hook by offering to let him live if he would just deny Christ. The great man would have none of it: 'Eighty-six years I have been his servant and he has done me no wrong. How can I then blaspheme my king who saved me?'

Quite a statement. His martyrdom has gone down in history and is recounted in the Letter of the Smyrnaeans. In that letter it is said that when the Romans tried to burn Polycarp to death the fire arched around him and they had to finish him off with a dagger.

His memory lives on. It certainly does and his qualities as a teacher have been proven too. Irenaeus, his disciple, became one of the most important church figures in the second century.

Most likely to say My date of Easter is the best.

Karl Rahner

Isn't he a modern theologian? He was; he died in 1984, but he had a huge impact on theology during this century. You almost certainly will have heard of 'anonymous Christians'. Well, that idea came from Rahner.

Who exactly was Rahner? He was a German theologian, born in 1904, and who later became a Jesuit. He was appointed to the theo-logical faculty at Innsbruck (where he studied) in 1936. He was made Professor after the Second World War and was also Professor at Munich and Münster Universities. He was influenced by the philosopher Heidegger and taught that divine grace can only be fully understood when it is experienced. But after Vatican II, where he was theological advisor, he developed the idea of 'anonymous Christians'.

What did he mean by that? It all goes back to the time of Cyprian, who taught that there was no salvation outside the Church. Pope Boniface VIII in 1302 put it even more bluntly: 'It is altogether necessary to salvation for every human creature to be subject to the Roman pontiff [pope].'

Rather a bold claim. Of course at that time the Church had split, so there was something of a political aspect to it. It has to be said that there have been many attempts to answer the question of what happens to the unbeliever.

How did Rahner get involved in that debate? The position of Pope Boniface might have been the official teaching of the Roman Catholic Church (indeed, technically it still is), but the Church states that it can be interpreted by the Church in different ways. So Pope Pius IX in 1854 said that this applied to everyone, except those who were ignorant of the Christian message, so long as they were not responsible for their ignorance. But this question of the state of the unbelievers would not go away.

And Rahner interpreted it anew for the Church? Yes, after an American priest tried to return to the traditional teaching, the Church said no one could interpret doctrine except the Church itself. Rahner, who wrote extensively, tried to explain the doctrine after Vatican II. So he taught that all people, at all times, had a real chance to believe.

Even if they had not heard the gospel? Exactly. Instead, the grace of Jesus Christ could reach them through their consciences, or even through a non-Christian religion. So even people who claim to be atheists can be saved because Christ is at work in their lives. They just don't realize it yet.

So that's why he called them 'Anonymous Christians'? Absolutely. He once wrote: 'The "anonymous Christian" in our sense of the term, is the pagan after the beginning of the Christian mission, who lives in the state of Christ's grace through faith, hope and love, yet who has no explicit knowledge of the fact that his life is orientated in grace-giving salvation to Jesus Christ.'

Has this line of thinking been influential? It has indeed. It has given rise to the idea that rather than seeing people as being lost, we should see them as being 'anonymous Christians'. This has also influenced Liberation Theology and even statements from groups like the World Council of Churches, because the Church is justified in refocusing her religious mission in favor of political injustices.

Least likely to say Only Christians are Christians.

Most likely to say Put an 'X' in the box for no publicity.

Nicholas Ridley

*W*asn't he a Conservative government minister? Not that one, this one was a famous bishop of London and a leading Reformer of the English church. He was a friend of Cranmer and helped him draw up the Book of Common Prayer.

A bishop of London, you say. When was that exactly? He was born in Northumberland in 1502 (we think) and went from there to study classics at Cambridge. But he continued his studies at the Sorbonne in Paris and at Louvain, and it is likely that he came face-to-face here with all of the Reforming ideas that were prevalent on the European continent. This was, after all, at the height of Luther's protests.

Did he come back to England after his studies? He certainly did. He came back to Cambridge where he was so enthused by all he had heard that he learned the New Testament epistles by heart.

That's not such a great achievement for a classics scholar. But in Greek? Anyway, in 1537 he was made chaplain to Cranmer and ten years later he was made bishop of Rochester. This was an important move because it gave him a seat in the House of Lords, and when they began discussing the Real Presence he made his views quite clear in the House. He had moved from the idea of transubstantiation to viewing the Eucharist as a spiritual feast.

The House of Lords debated it? Yes they did. It was an important subject at the time because it highlighted the rocky relationship between the Roman Catholic Church and the state. Ridley believed that the theology of transubstantiation was a novelty and it is thought that he based much of his thinking on a ninth-century work by a theologian called Ratramnus. Whatever, he was quite clear: 'I prefer the antiquity of the primitive church before the novelty of the Romish church,' he was to say.

How did all of this conclude? His main effort was to give backing to Archbishop Cranmer, but there were clearly people out to get him. It didn't stop his rise to power, though. In 1550 he was made bishop of London after Edward Bonner was deposed and imprisoned for disobeying a Privy Council order. He certainly made his mark there.

How? He wasted no time at all in throwing out the old stone altars in the churches of his new diocese and replacing them with wooden tables. He said: 'If we come to feed upon him, spiritually to eat his body and spiritually to drink his blood (which is the true use of the Lord's Supper), then no man can deny but the form of a table is more meet for the Lord's board than the form of an altar.'

It sounds like Ridley and Cranmer had things sewn up. All except for one detail. The monarchy. Ridley took a gamble and preached in favor of the accession of Lady Jane Grey to the throne, but when Mary succeeded his days were numbered. He was arrested almost immediately and thrown in jail, where he languished for eighteen months.

All for supporting the wrong candidate for Queen. He wasn't arrested for that, he was arrested for heresy. Some scholars think that the strategy was to get him to recant his Protestant ideas and thus to give a huge boost to Catholic teaching, but he would not recant. Indeed, when he was burned at the stake, along with Latimer in Balliol College, Oxford, he said: 'I cannot burn. Good people, let me have more fire.'

And did his ideas live on? They certainly did. He was influential in drafting the Book of Common Prayer and the forty-two Articles (which later were reduced to thirty-nine). But just as important, his concept of reformed Anglicanism was the one that modeled the Church of England from then on.

Don't mention Lady Jane Grey.

Do mention Greek Epistles.

ALBRECHT RITSCHL

An influential figure? Certainly. He lived from 1822 to 1889, but he has had a dramatic impact on theologians ever since. His main themes were on justification and ethical living, but his ideas were not altogether orthodox.

In what way? To begin to answer that we have to put his theology in context. He was reacting against Schleiermacher's emphasis on experience. Ritschl believed that this was too speculative and flimsy and that if there was any truth in the experiential line it had to be rooted in history somewhere. So, he said that Christian doctrine had to be traced back to the Bible, not just on what one was feeling on a particular day — that was too subjective. However, he complicated matters by arguing that religious views were little more than value judgments, so if it appealed to you then it was probably true. In saying this he was following in the footsteps of Immanuel Kant by associating religious views with value judgments rather than statements of fact.

Wasn't that a contradiction to what he said earlier? The key was that individuals could not make these value-judgements. The community of the Church was important, and what that community said was important. So rather than leaving everyone to work out their own salvation, he said that salvation was only available through the Church.

He therefore must have given the Church's doctrine a high place? No. For Ritschl most of the Church's teachers had viewed it wrong. Everyone, including the Reformers and even the early Church Fathers hadn't seen the light. But, relax, Ritschl was about to reveal all . . .

What was his solution? He denied original sin and so said that we could all live holy lives, if only we would try. This meant that what Jesus was doing was not paying back a debt to God, he was only showing us an example. Ritschl also upset some people by refusing to agree that Jesus had existed before he was born to Mary, and also questioning his true humanity. And, subsequently, he challenged the issue of Christ's resurrection, saying that he only lived on in the way he continued to influence people.

How did this affect his theology? He became one of the leading liberal theologians and of course from a practical point of view it meant that his theology, while highly moral, had a very temporal aspect to it. The question of the spiritual world and much of Christian orthodoxy was left wanting in his framework.

Did he not see anything special in religion? No, he believed that when you stripped away all the layers, every religious experience could be explained in other terms. So, for example, an answer to a prayer could simply be a coincidence, and so on.

Where was he teaching all of this? Ritschl, a pastor's son who was born in Berlin, later rose to become a bishop, studied at Bonn, Halle, Heidelberg and Tübingen before teaching at Bonn and Göttingen, where he remained from 1864 until his death.

And his works were influential? They certainly were; he has been described as perhaps the most influential theologian of his era in the liberal development of theology. Many other Protestant theologians picked up his ideas and they emerge in other places too.

Most likely to say Everyone's barking up the wrong tree.

Friedrich Schleiermacher

Sounds like a Formula 1 race car driver. No, but he has been called the father of Protestant theology, although not all Protestant theologians might agree with that.

Did he live at the time of the Reformation? No. He was born in Silesia in 1768, so he lived quite a long time after Luther, Calvin and co. He was brought up in a strict family but rebelled against it and went off to study at the University of Halle. It was here that he was introduced to the work of Kant and Aristotle, and soon after he was ordained to the priesthood. He has been described as a 'child of Romanticism'.

Why? Because his theology is based on feelings and emotions. This may have been a reaction against the strict upbringing he had or against the formalism of the German church at that time. It might also have been connected with the birth of Romanticism in the world generally, which suddenly put more emphasis on feelings.

And how did he work that into his theology? He taught that it wasn't so important what the Bible taught; what was of paramount importance was our consciousness of God, and of course that could vary from country to country and from religion to religion. Christianity, in his eyes, might be the best but it was not the only true religion.

How did this work out? He thought that if the Bible, or any authority, could not be relied on, what could be relied on was the sense of 'God-consciousness' in us all. If we depended on that we would be close to God. Conversely, sin was interpreted as not being dependent on this sense of God. Christ, for Friedrich, was the best example of this because he lived his life completely dependent on God. Although he had to admit that he didn't believe that Christ actually was God.

What was the reaction to this? Some scholars have claimed that Schleiermacher didn't so much found a school of thought as an era, so he was pretty important. It certainly fit in with the changing times. He felt that religion could survive if it was made a personal, inward discipline, rather than something that could be analyzed in the classroom. To discover the truth about it you had to start with yourself.

This was a new idea. It was new, but it fit in with the Romanticism of the era. He said: 'The sum total of religion is to feel that, in its highest unity, all that moves us in feeling is one; to feel that anything singular and particular is only possible by means of this unity; to feel, that is to say, that our being and living is a being and living in and through God.' It was all to do with feelings.

And how much of his thinking was due to his personal life? That depends on who you ask. He certainly was an intellectual thinker, but he also had a colorful private life. While he was brought up a pietist he rebelled against that. So much that when he fell in love with a married woman he tried to get her to leave her husband. When she didn't, he returned to teaching at Berlin. However, later in life he returned to his pious lifestyle, but in a way different from (and, he thought, better than) that of his parents.

Teaching at Berlin? But you said he was a priest. He was a priest, but after serving as chaplain at the Charite hospital in Berlin he went to become professor of theology at Halle. He left that seven years later to go back to Berlin and three years after that, in 1810, he was made dean of theology at the new university in Berlin.

Did he have any other achievements? Apart from all those books with impossible German titles? He played a leading part in the unification of the Lutheran and Reformed Churches in Prussia in 1817.

Your comments sound a little rude towards the Germans. Of course not. But Schleiermacher was a little rude about the English. He once said: 'Those proud islanders [the British] whom many unduly honor, know no watchword but gain and enjoyment. Their zeal for knowledge is only a sham fight, their worldly wisdom a false jewel, skillfully and deceptively composed, and their sacred freedom itself too often and too easily serves self-interest.'

Not to be confused with Schumacher.

CHARLES SIMEON

*A*chievement? He was the leader of the evangelical revival in England in the eighteenth and nineteenth centuries.

Was he a priest? Yes, after his education at Eton and King's College, Cambridge, he was ordained priest in 1783. He was at the same time appointed vicar to Holy Trinity, Cambridge, where he remained until he died.

If he led a revival, surely he had to do a lot of travelling? Well, his main influence was through the university. There, and in his parish, he experienced a lot of opposition to his message of personal conversion and systematic Bible teaching.

How did he respond to that? He was a kind, caring sort of person and his pastoral skills were brought to play. He was so successful in that that his opponents were won over. He soon was having a huge influence on undergraduates. He didn't do much travelling, despite the fact that he was deeply involved in the missionary movement.

How so? He was one of the people who set up the Church Missionary Society (as it was then known) and supported the British and Foreign Bible Society. Other groups, like the East India Company, had him as a consultant.

Were those his main achievements? No. He was also behind the Simeon Trustees who won the right to appoint priests to cleric benefices. When he died his Trust had the right to appoint twenty-one priests to a cleric benefice in the Church of England, mainly in large towns. One commentator points out that whereas in 1820 one in twenty Anglican clergy were evangelical, within ten years that had risen to one in eight. But his main achievement was to establish the evangelical party in the Church of England.

So he was somewhat of a politician then, getting the 'franchises' to parishes! You could say that, but his influence was much wider. The fact that groups like the East India Company consulted him about the appointment of chaplains shows that he was widely respected. Nevertheless, today's evangelicals have him to thank for securing their place in the Church.

Most likely to say I'm setting my sights on the world.

PIERRE TEILHARD DE CHARDIN

Now this sounds like a French theologian. Theologian and paleontologist.

Is that important? It certainly is. Pierre Teilhard de Chardin, who was born in rural France in 1881, joined the Jesuits and was ordained, but he was always interested in geology and palaeontology, and he found that as compelling as his religious calling. He was greatly influenced in the latter by his mother, who was deeply devoted to the Sacred Heart. In fact he was so torn between the two that he said they were like two 'rival stars'. So he tried to reconcile them by working on both.

Did they mix? He certainly thought so. He took up his scientific work with relish and was successful in it. In 1929 he celebrated helping to discover Peking Man – Sinanthropus – but this also led him to rethink the idea of evolution and how this related to his faith.

How did he reconcile the two? He came to the conclusion that the world was not exactly as we saw it. He believed that creation itself was the process of evolution and sin was just the by-product of that. He believed that we are all working our way to perfection and reconciliation with God, through Christ, whom he called the 'Omega Point'.

Omega Point? Yes, this Omega Point must be personal and absolute, and this is what Christ is. But mankind has a leading role to play in all of this. Whereas evolution continued in its own direction, when man came along he started to interfere with it and so we have to correct our mistakes. Nevertheless, history is moving to its climax in line with the will of God. And Omega, he believed, is Christ, who has a cosmological role to play.

This all sounds rather modern. It was a way of dealing with Darwin and his ideas of evolution, but it also fit in with the new development of Process Theology. This saw history on an evolutionary level, but Pierre wanted to merge the incarnation with evolution and this was his way of doing it.

Did he succeed? No. Not at first. He won much acclaim for his scientific work, but his Jesuit leaders were concerned about his teaching and banned him from publishing anything religious. When he died in 1955, at the age of seventy-four, his friends started publishing some of his work and it achieved a following then. It even influenced the Second Vatican Council.

And he came in from the cold. This was a major turnaround from the Church as they had earlier stopped him standing for a professorship at the Sorbonne, despite the fact that he had just been awarded the prestigious Legion of Honor for his academic work. The Catholic authorities never actually condemned his work, they just said it had to be read with caution. However, since Vatican II his influence has diminished somewhat.

Least likely to advocate Creation.

Most likely to advocate Evolution.

TERESA OF AVILA

She was a mystic, was she not? She was indeed, a Spanish one, who lived from 1515 to 1582, but she was as much a reformer as a mystic.

How so? Early on she had difficulties with her spiritual life, but after a profound experience she was then anxious to reform her Order.

She was a nun? Correct. Born into a long-established Spanish family, she was sent to a convent for education, but she felt a call to the monastic life. Her father was less than delighted, and brought her home at once. However, she then ran away and joined the Carmelite monastery at Avila.

Her dream achieved. One would have thought so, but in fact it only led to a sense of deep desolation. Her spiritual life suffered and the Rule of the convent proved to be too lax for her. All that changed in 1555 when she had a profound religious experience after meditating on a statue of Christ after he had been scourged. She said that she felt as if her heart had been broken and she placed all her trust in God.

That must have pleased her superiors. Not at first. Some of her confessors were worried that these experiences came from the devil rather than God.

Why? What was so unusual about that experience? Nothing on the surface, but soon afterwards she began to talk about the spiritual inner life and then she had her first 'ecstasy' and an intellectual vision of Christ. She talked about 'The Interior Castle', praying with the mind and spiritual marriage, all of which were regarded with some suspicion.

Was she worried about what was happening to her? She was certainly cautious. For example, she spoke about an experience in which an angel appeared before her carrying a spear tipped with fire. The angel plunged this spear into her heart, straight through to her innermost being. She was left ablaze with a love for God. However, while she talked about these experiences she never stressed them because she recognized their dangers as well as their value.

Did she believe that experiences such as these were for every Christian? All of this was going on against the background of the Reformation. In other parts of Europe the Protestants were seeing people respond to their message, what she was doing was offering a more emotional faith as opposed to the intellectual sort that was more generally available. So yes, she believed that every Christian could have a personal relationship with God.

How did the Church authorities respond? With horror. On the surface she was undermining the priests, and there was also talk, perhaps too much talk, about her religious ecstasies as embarrassing or even erotic. But they were also concerned at her efforts to reform her Order, to make it stricter and more faithful to the original Rule. They had nothing to lose but their shoes, she said. And on top of all that, she was eager to heal the division with Protestants.

Quite a task for a single woman. Yes, but Teresa was a strong woman, who was shrewd and with great practical abilities. She found an avid follower in John of the Cross and the two of them had immense success in their mission. While the papal nuncio in Spain called her a 'restless gadabout', she founded 16 religious houses, was canonized in 1622 and was declared a Doctor of the Church in 1970.

Most likely to say Don't imagine that if you had a great deal of time you would spend more of it in prayer. Get rid of that idea! Again and again God gives more in a moment than in a long period of time, for his actions are not measured by time at all.

TERTULLIAN

An early church theologian? Most certainly. Quintus Septimius Florens Tertullian, to give him his full name, was born in Carthage in what is now Tunis around the year 160. We do know that before the year 197 he had become a Christian and he was one of the most important Christians between the time of the Apostle Paul and Augustine in the fourth century.

What was important about him? If you have ever used the word 'Trinity' to talk about the Father, Son and Holy Spirit, you have Tertullian to thank. For it was he who coined that phrase. This was because he was the first major theologian to write in Latin and many of his terms have remained with us to the present day.

Was there an argument about the Trinity then? Yes there was. There was a sect called the Monarchians, who stressed the monarchy of God and maintained that God was 'one'. They came up with the idea that there was only one person of the Godhead, it was just that he carried out different functions. So at the present he might be God the Father, later he would act as God the Son and tomorrow he might do something as God the Holy Spirit, but it was the same person each time. Tertullian refuted this and he rebutted them by saying that God is one substance in three persons. This was a major development in the Church's battle with heretics.

Quite an achievement. And he was also the first to write a theological work about baptism and the first to write a Christian book on psychology. His *On Baptism* is the earliest work we have on the subject; however, in it he is against infant baptism, because he believed that at baptism a great chasm was crossed and Christians did not need to sin after that. Indeed, he believed that sin committed after baptism was unforgivable. He was afraid that children might sin without realizing it and so threaten their eternal salvation.

He was a prolific writer. He was. We can divide up his work into three categories: the first were apologetic works, the most famous of these being his *Apology*. This book was aimed at the Romans and defended the right of Christians to play their part in society. One of his most famous quotes comes from this: 'If the Tiber reaches the walls, if the Nile does not rise, if the sky does not move or if the earth does, if there is famine or plague, the cry is "To the lions with the Christians." What! So many of them to one lion?'

Strong stuff. It was indeed. And it was true to say that Tertullian took no prisoners in his battles with his opponents. He was a clever man who had to show his opponents as being completely wrong, and he did. It was said that even the pagans read his books because they were so entertaining.

What else did he write? Well, after the apologetic works, there were books written against the heretics and the books on practical and ethical matters. In the books against heresy he could be rhetorical. For example, he seemed to have no time for philosophy, saying that it was of the devil and the root of all heresy. Nevertheless, he did employ it from time to time. His famous question, 'What has Athens got to do with Jerusalem', sums up that way of thinking.

And his practical works? He was something of an ascetic and, perhaps not unusual at a time when it was the norm for Christians to rise from their beds at midnight to pray, he encouraged a life of purity and abstinence. He even challenged Pope Callistus, whom he thought was being too lenient in disciplining sexual sin. But some of this may have been connected with his flirtation with Montanism.

What was that? It was a movement some thought heretical, and was branded as such by the Pope. Tertullian was attracted to it because it stressed purity and discipline, but it also had apocalyptic features. It was perhaps the charismatic movement of the day as it stressed the ministry of the Paraclete and ecstatic prophecy. It also taught no second marriage, greater austerity and no flight from persecution. However, whatever criticism they made of Tertullian, his theology remained scriptural right up until his death from old age sometime after the year 220.

Did his influence outlive him? Absolutely. He was described as the 'Father of Latin Theology' and he is still widely regarded today. He is said to be one of the greatest Latin writers ever and one person even commented that he was 'incapable of being dull'.

Most likely to say These Romans have got it in for us.

HELMUT THIELICKE

Sounds like a classic German theologian. And he was, in more ways than one. Helmut Thielicke was born in 1908 in the town of Barmen. He became a professor of theology at Heidelberg after studying theology at many German universities, but when he attacked the Nazis he was dismissed from his post in 1940.

What did he do then? He actually spent a brief period in the army. He didn't go abroad as many did at the time to escape the Nazis, but when he came out of the army he became a Lutheran priest. When the war ended he resumed his academic career, only this time he went to Tübingen, where he was professor of systematic theology.

Other theologians spoke out against the Nazis, didn't they? Yes, Paul Tillich attacked them for their racism, saying that race and class were being made into idols; Bonhoeffer likewise attacked the Nazis, but he came to a tragic end. Barth opposed them, but he got off lightly at first because he was Swiss. Thielicke told them that their quest would end in tears because independence from God could only result in meaninglessness. He survived to tell the tale.

Where did he stand theologically? He was fairly conservative, but he preferred to mark the distinction between liberals and conservatives in Cartesian and non-Cartesian terms.

Whatever did he mean by that? He thought that people like Bultmann, Tillich and Schleiermacher, for example, started off at the wrong point. They were Cartesian theologians. This term came from Descartes and he meant by this that they started their theological quest with man. He shared their concern to relate the gospel message to modern man, but Thielicke believed they went too far and that they gave modern man the veto when it came to interpreting God.

The veto? Yes, if man is perceived to be so advanced, then we can only accept interpretations about God that are logical to us. It rules out any revelation from God that does not conform to laws of physics or biology or chemistry, or whatever. So man controls theological study; for Thielicke this was wrong.

Was he an ivory-tower theologian? Not at all, he lived very much in the real world. He once commented: 'Tell me how much you know of the sufferings of your fellow men and I will tell you how much you have loved them.' So you can see that he was concerned for people.

So he was a non-Cartesian? Well anticipated. He saw two dangers with theology, one was to be so conservative that we 'go on preaching with an artificially preserved naïveté as if we were still living in the sixteenth century'. The other danger was that some theologians were so determined to reinterpret everything they were 'practically drowning in hermeneutical reflection'. So he tried to navigate between these two extremes.

Did he succeed? Some would say he did, that he found a way of interpreting the faith to modern man without losing the essential message. He wrote many books, among which were a substantial number of devotional works, and a book on *Theological Ethics*, which was trying to apply biblical teaching to modern dilemmas.

Famous quote Man becomes a holy thing, a neighbor, only if we realize that he is the property of God and that Jesus Christ died for him.

Most likely to say We need a *via media* in theology.

PAUL TILLICH

What era are we in here, then? Paul Tillich was a twentieth-century theologian. He was born in Germany in 1886 and taught in five different German universities. However, his experiences as an army chaplain in the First World War (where he received the Iron Cross) affected him deeply. He later became sympathetic with the left wing and when a certain Adolf Hitler appeared on the scene in Germany things got tight for him.

What happened? Hitler had him banned from teaching because he was associated with the 'Religious Socialists'. Tillich was proud of this, claiming that he had been the first non-Jew 'to be so honored'. Anyway, he decided to cut his losses and move to America.

Did he get a job there? Yes, thanks to Reinhold Niebuhr he became professor of philosophical theology at Union Theological Seminary in New York, and he remained there until he retired in 1955, although he carried on lecturing until his death ten years later.

And what was his theology? Very progressive. He disagreed with Barth and others and invented a new kind of thinking, which he called the 'method of correlation'. He meant by this that it was pointless talking about eternal truths without grounding them in the current context. So he attacked orthodoxy for its dependence on the past. He wanted the Church to answer the questions people were asking today. In doing this he wanted to bridge the gap between modern culture and Christian belief.

What exactly was this 'method of correlation'? Well, you have to start with the questions that modern people are asking and then give answers based on eternal truths.

That hardly sounds controversial. As a method it was not, but some theologians think that Tillich fell into the trap he was exposing, and that he undermined the eternal truths of Christianity. He went so far as to say that one couldn't say that God exists.

Now that's what I call controversial. Yes, but he had a serious point. He maintained that God was so great that to talk about him existing was to minimize the status of God. So, he argued, God was 'Being-itself' and while God was personal, he believed that God was not a person as such. He was far bigger than our understanding would allow.

So he wasn't an atheist? Probably not, but he did have many problems with the traditional orthodox Christian belief about the nature of God. He was adamant that many people dismissed the idea of God, thinking that they had thought about him seriously, when all the time they had never come close to encountering the 'Ultimate'. For the Church to say that 'God exists' is too weak, for it puts God on the same level as everyday objects.

How did that go over with the Church? It wasn't popular, partly because Tillich had a habit of encouraging people to question the creeds and councils of the Church. But that didn't bother him much. One of his guiding ideas was 'accept the fact that you are accepted [by God]', so whether the church authorities approved of him or not did not matter much to him.

Was he influential? Yes, he was. And that for him was a good thing. He once said that 'In the depth of anxiety of having to die is the anxiety of being eternally forgotten.' In other words, the worst thing that can happen to us is that people ignore us. It is too early to say whether Tillich will be eternally remembered, but since his death at the age of seventy-nine his ideas have lived on. He was a major influence in the *Honest to God* book of John A. T. Robinson and some see traces of his thought in the work of Don Cupitt, particularly his book *Taking Leave of God*.

What about his own books? His main work was three volumes of *Systematic Theology*, which he published in 1951–64. However, he was prolific, and some of his books began as talks or sermons.

Least likely to say Never question the Church.

WILLIAM TYNDALE

He was a Bible translator, wasn't he? Yes, he was. In fact, he was the first person to print a translation of the New Testament into English. There was an earlier version, translated by Wycliffe, but this had inaccuracies, as it had been translated from the Latin Vulgate. Tyndale translated his New Testament from the original Greek.

What drove him to this project? Born in Gloucestershire around 1495, he graduated from Oxford and Cambridge and took a job as a tutor in the house of Sir John Walsh at Little Sodbury, near Bath. While he was there he grew furious at the ignorance of the local clergy and said: 'If God spare my life, ere many years pass, I will cause a boy that driveth the plough shall know more of the Scriptures than thou dost.' And he did.

He must have been quite a hero. To many he was more of a zero than a hero. Thomas More called him the 'captain of English heretics' and there was so much opposition to his work that he had to flee to Germany, never to return.

Why was he so unpopular? The bishops were so concerned to stop the spread of Lutheran ideas that they refused to support him. Undeterred, he got backing from London tradesmen, but things were getting intense here, and that was when he left for Germany.

He had an easier time there? Not quite. While his New Testament was on the presses at Cologne the authorities became aware of it and raided the presses. Tyndale managed to escape in time, taking his pages with him. The following year, 1526, his first complete New Testament was finally printed in the German town of Worms and was smuggled into Britain at the end of the year by a sort of forerunner of Brother Andrew.

What happened then? At the beginning Tyndale had tried to get backing from the bishop of London, Cuthbert Tunstall, but he was dead set against it. So when the first Bibles turned up he had a ceremonial burning of them at St Paul's Cross. Then Archbishop Warham (of Canterbury) bought up most of the remaining copies and burned them. This only served to help Tyndale, for it paid for a further printing.

So he only translated the New Testament? At first, yes, but he later translated the first five books of the Old Testament from the Hebrew, then Jonah and the books Joshua to 2 Chronicles. He was able to do all of this because his mentor at Cambridge, Erasmus, had translated the Greek New Testament.

If there was so much opposition, how come he is so highly regarded nowadays? It may have had something to do with Tyndale himself. In 1535, when he was just forty-one, he was betrayed by a fellow Englishman at Antwerp, where he was strangled and burned at the stake the following year. His last words were: 'Lord, open the king of England's eyes.' This prayer was answered because Henry VIII then authorized the publication of an English translation of the Bible. The versions that followed were closely based on Tyndale's work.

Such as? Around ninety per cent of the King James Version is based on Tyndale, and seventy-five per cent of the Revised Standard Version is accredited to him. So while all the church figures here were furious at first they soon changed their tune. In 1537 the first Bible actually to be printed in England was produced. It had on it the name 'Thomas Matthew', who was a co-worker of Tyndale. Then Coverdale produced his version, again largely based on Tyndale's work, and one of the people who examined it for the king was none other than Cuthbert Tunstall. This time he said it was rather good.

Don't mention Cuthbert Tunstall.

JAMES USSHER

idn't he have funny ideas about the creation of the world? He did cal-culate that the world was created in the year 4004 BC, and at the time his calculation was widely regarded as being accurate. So much so that the date was added to the margins of Bibles in 1701, and remained there for two centuries.

We can laugh about it now, but was he off in his reasoning? On the contrary, Archbishop Ussher (he was Archbishop of Armagh in Ireland) was one of the cleverest people in the whole of Europe and he was highly regarded as a theologian, a chronologist and as an expert in antiquity. He may have got the date wrong about the creation of the world, but he more than redeemed himself with Ignatius.

What's he got to do with it? Well, there were a number of fake letters from Ignatius of Antioch making the rounds. Their existence meant that theolo-gians refused to accept that any of them were genuine. Ussher correctly iden-tified seven that were the real McCoy and became a real authority on these.

But if he got the date of creation wrong, was he to be trusted on these? It could have been a forerunner of the Hitler Diaries, especially as the ver-sions he was working from were found in England. However, when a Greek manuscript was discovered in Florence, it proved him right and he was the hero of the known world.

So he was something of a scholar. More than something. He was ordained in 1601, when he was just twenty and five years later he was made chan-cellor of St Patrick's Cathedral. The following year he was made the first professor of divinity at Dublin, where he was one of their first students, but turned down an offer to be the provost there because, he said, it would interfere with his studies.

And was he highly regarded or just eager? Very highly regarded. One of his contemporaries called him a 'giant among giants'.

What was his theology? He was a Calvinist and tried to get the Lambeth Articles introduced to the Church in Ireland. These were the forerunners of the thirty-nine Articles and were significantly more Calvinist in tone than the thirty-nine. In the event he was overruled, but it shows where his theology was coming from.

Did that affect his standing in the Church? Not a lot. However, after the Irish rebellion of 1641 he stayed on in Britain and it is testament to his character that while he was a loyalist to the monarchy he was so highly regarded that Cromwell ordered that he should have a state funeral in Westminster Abbey when he died in 1656.

Most likely to say I know exactly when the world was created.

JOHN WESLEY

*T*he hymn-singing founder of Methodism? Yes, but don't get John confused with his brother Charles, who wrote most of the hymns. Both were sons of an Anglican clergyman in Epworth, Lincolnshire, but it was John who led the movement.

How did it start? John became a Christian a few days after his brother on May 24, 1738, when he heard Luther's preface to Romans being read at a religious society in Aldersgate Street, London. He said that his heart had been 'strangely warmed'. The Anglican's evangelistic fire was stirred and he got to work preaching the message.

So why did he become a Methodist? That was due to the displeasure of the Anglican Church with his enthusiasm. Bristol's Bishop Butler reflected the general displeasure with the Wesleys and banned John from evangelizing in his diocese.

Too enthusiastic? And his enthusiasm never waned. By the end of his life he had travelled over 200,000 miles and preached over 40,000 sermons, mostly in the open air. But he nevertheless suffered mob violence as well as clergy hostility.

So he wasn't your typical parish priest? Certainly not, and when people complained that he never stayed long in one area he replied that the world was his parish.

So he set up his own church? He never wanted to leave the Church of England, but he was forced to develop a network of local preachers, covering the whole of the country by 1751. He always saw Methodism as a renewal movement within the Church, but he managed to reach many ordinary working people who felt left out of the Church.

What were his beliefs? He preached justification by faith but linked this with the pursuit of holiness, leading to the doctrine of Christian perfection. This was a subsequent experience after salvation and he taught that believers have sin permanently removed from them.

And as we know, his movement was successful. Yes, by the time of his death in 1791, at the age of eighty-eight, Methodists numbered 72,000 in Great Britain and Ireland and 57,000 in North America.

Not to be confused with Charles Wesley.

Don't mention Bishops.

Do mention Holiness, singing and evangelism.

JOHN WYCLIFFE

The first man to translate the Bible into English? He probably didn't actually translate it himself, but even if he didn't he was still the main impetus behind it. This was due to his belief that ordinary people should be able to read it for themselves, not just the priests. It was part of a range of views that he held which caused controversy during his short life.

How short? He was born in 1330 and died from a stroke in 1384. Originally from a propertied family in Yorkshire, he soon went to Oxford where he had a distinguished academic career. That all came to a bitter end when Archbishop Langham expelled him, preferring in his place to turn the post over to a monastic establishment. Wycliffe sued but ended up going to a parish instead. However, he was well connected during this time and carried out some work for the Royal Court. He was particularly friendly with John of Gaunt and worked as a sort of medieval spin-doctor for the government.

All the while he was still a priest? Yes, it was fairly common in those times for someone to hold the living of a parish and to benefit from the income without actually carrying out any of the duties. And this is what he did.

Was the Church upset by that? No, no, no. What they were upset with was his attack on them. Having originally made his name as a philosopher, Wycliffe now turned to theology and found inspiration from the Bible and early Church Fathers. The first of his comments to attract opposition was that leaders could only lead by grace. So, when people turned into evil leaders, they no longer had any authority to lead. This, he went on, applied equally to secular and to religious leaders.

What was the outcome of that? The monasteries were full of people who had made vows of poverty yet the Church was exceedingly rich; estimates were that the Church owned up to a third of the land in England yet still evaded paying tax. The government was very interested in what Wycliffe was saying. After all, they had a war against France to finance.

Popular with the government but not with the Church. You can imagine them eating their own words. The Pope, Gregory XI, reacted quickly, at the request of the English clergy, and condemned this teaching. However, Wycliffe had influential friends who protected him from attack. Nevertheless, it seemed that the reformer was just getting ready, for his next move outraged the Church even more.

What did he say? He condemned the theology of transubstantiation, saying that it was not logical, scriptural and was even philosophically questionable. Wycliffe also said that because the Church was made up of the redeemed, there was no need for priests to intercede for them or to forgive them for sins.

Did he have a death wish? His ideas were suggestive of what the Reformers would say after him, but he wasn't saying all of this just to be provocative, he genuinely believed that the Church had been in error and needed to reform itself urgently. But while others attacked practices like indulgences he went deeper than that and attacked the theology behind such practices.

Did he face prosecution? Not directly. However, when he made his comments about the Eucharist, this proved too much for his colleagues at Oxford. They condemned him and he was forced out. He went back to his parish in Lutterworth and gathered around him a small band of followers. Many of those were to pay with their lives for following him, but Wycliffe was able to die in his bed.

Where did the Bible translation come in? He believed that everyone should be able to read the Bible and this is why he had it translated from the Vulgate (Latin) version. He also established 'poor preachers' who went around the country preaching the gospel and reading the Bible.

How influential was he? In the immediate period he was greatly influential with his policy of translating the Bible into the vernacular. He also had a huge impact on Jan Hus, the Czech theologian. His followers outlived him, and they came to be known as 'Lollards' (which is a Dutch word meaning 'mumblers').

And he had a peaceful death? He did, but he was condemned at the Council of Constance and his bones were dug up and burned in 1428.

FRANCIS XAVIER

Didn't he help found the Jesuits? He did indeed, along with Ignatius Loyola. Xavier was born in Spain to a noble family, and when Ignatius met him at the University of Paris he recognized that this bright, handsome and cheerful young man could be a great Christian. The two of them joined forces to set up the Society of Jesus (Jesuits) and they made their vows of poverty and obedience. The new vow they added to their Society's vows was to obey the Pope in whatever he said.

And did they? Did they ever. When the Portuguese ambassador asked the Pope (John III) to send missionaries to evangelize the East, Francis set off at two days' notice. He was eminently successful too – the Jesuits estimate that during his short life (he died when he was only forty-six) he converted 700,000 people.

All in the East? Yes, he was known as the Apostle of the Indies (and Japan). He sailed from Lisbon in 1541 and a year later he arrived in Goa. From there he preached and baptized in what is now Vietnam, Malaysia and China. In Japan he established a Christian community that still exists today.

What were his secrets? He described his methods in South India as follows: on Sundays he assembled all the people, got them to say prayers in their own language, he gave out the first commandment, which they all repeated and then they said a prayer. After that they recited the Pater Noster, the Ave Maria and then continued through the other nine commandments.

What was his theology? He was a reforming Catholic, but he was strongly opposed to the Protestants. Ordained a priest in 1537 he lived in Rome to do whatever the Society or Pope asked of him. Some theologians believe that he was thoroughly medieval in his views and equated the glory of

God with the glory of Portugal, and so on. However, he was not just concerned to evangelize where the Portuguese empire extended, he went to the extremes to preach the gospel. This despite the fact that he suffered terribly from seasickness.

And was he successful? A year after he arrived at Goa he went to Travancore, where he baptized 10,000 converts. He travelled all over the East, and in Ceylon he even converted the King of Kandy. On his way to Canton in China he died and his body was returned to Goa, from where he had set out. It remains there where the people venerate it.

Famous quote Give me the children until they are seven and anyone may have them afterwards.

Least likely to say I like the Reformers' ideas.

ULRICH ZWINGLI

His name rings a bell. Wasn't he a Reformer? If he hadn't met an early death on the battlefield, some theologians say we would be talking about Zwinglians instead of Calvinists. He was, after all, the man who started the Reformation in Switzerland.

How did he come to have such an important role? Coming from a peasant background, he was highly intelligent and went into the Church. One of his first jobs was to go as chaplain to Swiss mercenaries in Italy. That was a formative experience on him and on his return he started preaching in his parish church against the mercenary business. This did not go over well, for it was a lucrative source of income for the Swiss. It's like telling the Swiss today that banking is a sin.

So he made some enemies. Yes, and he was moved from that job, eventually ending up at the Gross Münster (Great Cathedral) in Zurich. Perhaps they thought he would be overawed by the move and keep quiet. It was here he started to preach systematically through the Bible. This was a common practice in the early Church, but it was seen as radical when Zwingli reintroduced it.

Was this when his reforms started? Yes, by 1522 he started writing about his reforming ideas, in 1523 he even got a letter of approval from the Pope, but things changed after the Mass was abolished in Zurich in 1525.

Did he suffer much opposition? Yes, he most certainly did, not only from the church authorities but also from other reforming groups. The Anabaptists formed themselves into the first free church at this time, but the most serious opposition came from the Lutherans (whom Zwingli dismissed, along with the Papists, as those 'who long for the flesh pots of Egypt').

Why did he dislike the Lutherans so much? The dispute was over the Mass.

Luther taught consubstantiation, the real presence of Christ in the Mass (but still not transubstantiation), but Zwingli maintained that there was no question of any physical presence. But Calvin also disagreed with him. He maintained that it was not just a symbol: Christ is present, but only in a spiritual way.

Were they divided on anything else? The question of baptism was crucial. Some did not like the idea of a reformed state church, they wanted a voluntary church whose members were admitted by adult baptism. Here again Zwingli split with Luther (and the Catholics) by teaching that baptism was primarily an outward sign of faith, rather than bestowing new birth on individuals.

Interesting theological arguments. It was much more than that. Zwingli believed that the state had the right to rule on religious matters and when the council put some of the Anabaptist leaders to death by drowning, Zwingli said nothing. So it was much more than an obscure theological point. Ask the Anabaptists.

Harsh times, the Middle Ages. They certainly were, and no less for Zwingli himself. He tried to set up a network of evangelical cantons in Switzerland, but the Catholic Church objected and war eventually followed. Zwingli was killed on the battlefield in Keppel in 1531, at the age of only forty-seven. The reforming work he started was left to Calvin to continue.

Least likely to say Let's agree to differ.

Most likely to say Don't call it Mass.

GLOSSARY

39 Articles A list of doctrinal beliefs accepted by the Church of England as defining orthodoxy.

Agnostics People who believe that one cannot know if there is a God or not.

Allegory Narrative used to identify another reality.

Allegorical Method Interpreting the Bible by identifying the spiritual realities symbolized there. This arose as a reaction against a literal reading of the text.

Anamnesis Memorial.

Anathema A formal curse by a pope or church council denouncing a doctrine.

Apocrypha A group of books accepted from an early date as canonical, but nevertheless controversial because they do not appear in the Hebrew Old Testament. Many do not recognize them as canonical, but the Roman Catholic Church does.

Apologetics The defense of Christian beliefs.

Apostles From the Greek word *apostello* meaning to send. It referred originally to the disciples but in Hebrews 3:11, it also referred to Christ.

Atonement The reconciliation of man to God through the sacrifice of Christ. It literally means 'at-one-ment'.

Canon (1) A recognized collection of books comprising Holy Scripture. (2) In the Middle Ages 'canon law' came to distinguish church law from secular law. (3) Member of clergy associated with a cathedral or collegiate church. (4) A decree.

Canons In the Church of England, this is the main body of church law.

Cappadocian Fathers St Basil the Great, St Gregory of Nazianzus and St Gregory of Nyssa are known as the Cappadocian Fathers after their birthplace. They succeeded in defeating Arianism.

155

Catholic General or universal. Since the Reformation it has been used by the Roman church, particularly, to refer to the Roman Church alone.

Christology The study of the person of Christ.

Church Father Figures such as Tertullian and Origen were cited from the time of the Cappadocian Fathers as proofs of orthodoxy. Not all the so-called Fathers (dating from the first five centuries) were orthodox and the term has more use as a popular term than as an official church appellation.

Communion Sharing. (1) Holy Communion is another term for the Eucharist or Mass. (2) Meaning the fellowship of Christians, e.g. Communion of saints, the body of Christ.

Confirmation A religious rite that confirms the gift of the Holy Spirit at Baptism.

Council A meeting of bishops from the Church worldwide to regulate practice or doctrine. The **General Council** is held to be the highest human authority for the Church. Local, national or denominational meetings are usually known as 'synods' or some other term.

Counter Reformation Beginning at the time of Luther, this was a movement to reinvigorate and reform the Roman Catholic Church, also known as the Roman Reformation.

D A term used to define the Documentary Hypothesis, that the Pentateuch was compiled from four sources, J, E, D and P. The 'D' classification refers to almost all of the book of Deuteronomy.

Deacon Servant or minister. In church order, this role comes after bishop and priest (or 'presbyter') see Acts 6:1–6.

Diet A legislative assembly.

Doctor of the Church A title given to outstanding Christian theologians. The list contains thirty names, but the four pre-eminent Doctors are: Gregory the Great, Ambrose, Augustine of Hippo and Jerome.

Donatists A North African schismatic group from the 4th to the 17th century who believed that only those who lived holy lives were Christians.

E A term used to define the Documentary Hypothesis, that the Pentateuch was compiled from four sources, J, E, D and P. The 'E' term refers to passages that use the word 'Elohim' for God, and scholars think this came later than the J passages.

Election The act of God in choosing people. The term was popularized by Augustine but it was Calvin who stressed God's part in choosing people, irrespective of merit or works.

Elizabethan Settlement A term referring to the full establishment of the Church of England (during the years 1559–63) under the reign of Elizabeth I.

Enabling Act A law passed in 1919 by the British Parliament that allows the Church of England to order its own affairs, subject to the control of Parliament.

Eucharist From the Greek word *eucharistia*, meaning 'thanksgiving'. It refers in Christian practice to Holy Communion.

Evangelical From the Greek word *euangelion*, meaning 'good news'. The term now refers to those churches and Christians who stress the necessity of teaching the Gospel of Christ as a means of salvation.

Father Originally a title given to bishops, it is now used widely as a term for priests.

Form criticism The process to get behind the original structure of biblical texts, particularly, to get the oral stage of the Gospel tradition.

Homoiousion A Greek word, meaning 'of like substance'.

Homoousion A Greek word, meaning 'of one substance'.

Hypostasis A Greek word whose meaning was the cause of much debate.

J A term used to define the Documentary Hypothesis, that the Pentateuch was compiled from four sources, J, E, D and P. The 'J' term refers to those passages that use the word 'Jehovah' (hence 'J') or YHWH to refer to God.

Justification The process of man being declared righteous in the eyes of God.

Koran The sacred book of the Islamic faith.

Liberation theology A movement that developed among Roman Catholic theologians in Latin America in the 1960s and that advocated dealing with physical as well as spiritual poverty.

Mass A Latin term for the liturgical celebration of the Eucharist.

Myth A traditional story, often involving a supernatural element, but not necessarily untrue.

Nicene Creed Originally from the Council of Nicaea (AD 325), this set of beliefs was designed to counter Arianism; but a slightly different form, missing out the anathemas, is commonly used in churches today.

Nonconformity The refusal to conform to the doctrines and dogma of any established church. The term originally referred to those who refused to accept the authority of the Church of England but is now applied to dissenters in general.

Oath of Allegiance An oath that Church of England clergy make to the monarch, acknowledging the sovereign as Supreme Governor of the Church of England.

Oecumenical A Greek word, referring to 'the inhabited world', now refers to the whole Christian world. The modern spelling 'ecumenical' is more commonly used. The Archbishop of Constantinople is known as the Oecumenical Patriarch.

Oratory From the Latin 'oratorium', meaning place of prayer.

P A term used to define the Documentary Hypothesis, that the Pentateuch was compiled from four sources, J, E, D and P. The 'P' strand is said to contain the 'Priestly' (hence 'P') material. Some scholars claim that it contains the latest material in the Pentateuch.

Patriarch A word referring to the father or leader of a tribe. Abraham, Isaac and Jacob are the three most famous patriarchs. In Christian terms it means the bishops of Rome, Alexandria, Antioch, Constantinople and Jerusalem. In recent times the term has been awarded to leaders of self-governing churches in the East.

Pentateuch The first five books of the Old Testament: Genesis, Exodus, Leviticus, Numbers and Deuteronomy.

Predestination The doctrine as to who is 'foreordained' to salvation.

Prevenient The activity of the Holy Spirit in bringing God's grace to people at the point of making a choice about salvation.

Protestant The term dates from the issuing of a decree by five princes and fourteen cities in 1529 protesting at the lack of reforms in the Church; it was later used to contrast Lutheran (Protestant) with Calvinist (Reformed). In the modern world the term is all-embracing for those who are not Roman Catholic or Orthodox. Protestant beliefs often include a high regard for the Bible as the only authority for church life, the priesthood of all believers and a stress on the doctrine of justification by faith alone.

Puritans English Protestants who were unhappy with the Elizabethan Settlement and wanted further reform along the lines of Calvin's Geneva model. They demanded explicit scriptural warrant for any church practice and rejected all else as superstition, popish or anti-Christian. Consequently they placed emphasis on a table for Holy Communion rather than an altar, and on Sunday observance, and opposed vestments, icons and the sign of the cross.

Q From the German word *Quelle*, meaning 'source', it is used by some scholars to identify a source for various passages in the Synoptic Gospels. It is believed that Q is a separate document that was used by the Gospel writers to compile their accounts of the life of Christ.

Real Presence The doctrine that the bread and wine in the Eucharist do actually become the body and blood of Christ.

Reformation A general term referring to a variety of changes in church life between the 14th and 17th centuries. It is believed to have begun with the Lollards, but it also found expression through Martin Luther, Ulrich Zwingli and John Calvin. The movement for reform swept through Europe and nearly every country was affected.

Romanticism The 18th-century move away from rationalism in Europe. It fed the theology of Schleiermacher and Coleridge in its flight from the Enlightenment.

Sacred Heart The devotion to the human heart of Jesus. It is thought to have emerged from the account of the wound on Christ's side. Since 1765 it has been a feast of the Roman Catholic Church.

Scholasticism A form of theological inquiry that operates by positing two contradictory statements and applying logic to uncover the synthesized meaning inherent in the two statements.

Stigmata The reproduction of the wounds of Christ on the human body.

Synod A council of the church.

Synoptic Gospels Matthew, Mark and Luke are referred to as synoptic Gospels because they report the life of Christ in a similar, systematic way in comparison to the more personal, narrative style of John.

Theotokos A Greek word, meaning 'God bearer', a title for the Virgin Mary.

Unitarian A belief that rejects the divinity of Christ and denies the Trinity.

Venerable In the Roman Catholic Church this is a description of a deceased person at one stage of the canonization process. In the Church of England the term refers to archdeacons.

WCC The World Council of Churches.